The Cornerstones of Prosperity

Emmanuel Adewusi

CCCG Publishing House

Copyright © 2024 Emmanuel Adewusi

All rights reserved. No part of this book may be used or reproduced by any means, graphics, electronic, or mechanical, including photocopying, recording, taping, or by any information storage retrieval system without the author's written permission except in cases of brief quotations embodied in critical articles and reviews.

Scriptures are taken from the New King James Version. Copyright 1979, 1980, 1982 by Thomas Nelson, Inc. Used by permission. All right reserved.

Author: Emmanuel Adewusi

ISBN: 978-1-989099-36-0 (hardcover)

ISBN: 978-1-989099-37-7 (ebook)

First Printing 2024

Contents

Dedication	IV
Preface	V
Introduction	VII
1. The Cornerstones of Prosperity	1
2. How to Identify Opportunities to Prosper	18
3. How to Take Advantage of Opportunities	29
4. How to Escape Poverty	37
5. The Blessings of The Lord	53
6. Manifesting Prosperity	65
Epilogue	79
Contact the Author	81
A Sinner's Prayer	82
About the author	83

Dedication

This book is dedicated to all those who believe they are ready to be custodians of wealth for the purpose of advancing the Church of Jesus Christ from coast to coast. May the content of this book become flesh in your life. May the Lord grant you access to the treasures of darkness, and hidden riches of secret places. May your relationship with Jesus, the Head of the Church, go deeper and deeper in Jesus' mighty name.

Preface

It is with great joy and anticipation that I welcome you to the pages of this book, dedicated to exploring the divine principles of financial prosperity within the context of our faith. I am passionate about unveiling scriptural truths that empower us to live lives of abundance and fulfillment according to God's promises. Prosperity is a divine inheritance bestowed upon God's beloved children. It is important to align our lives with the fundamental principles of prosperity outlined in Scripture, recognizing that true abundance transcends mere monetary wealth.

As we embark on this transformative journey together, I fervently desire to challenge preconceived notions and dispel misconceptions surrounding the topic of prosperity within the Body of Christ. We must confront the sensitivities and hesitations that often accompany discussions on this subject, acknowledging the profound implications of poverty and lack while embracing a vision of abundance that aligns with the promises of our Heavenly Father.

Throughout the following pages, we will delve deeper into the scriptural foundations of prosperity, drawing insights from the lives of biblical personalities and the timeless wisdom contained within the Word of God. We will explore the principles of tithing, sacrificial giving, and generosity, uncovering the transformative power of stewardship and obedience in unlocking God's abundant blessings. I pray that this book serves as a beacon of hope and inspiration, guiding you on a journey of discovery and empowerment as you uncover your financial inheritance in Christ. May you be equipped with the knowledge and wisdom to take hold of God's promises and walk confidently in the path of prosperity, He has ordained for His beloved children.

Introduction

Prosperity is one of those things that people desire but feel guilty for desiring. I will tell you right out the gate that your Heavenly Father wants you to be financially prosperous. The extent of prosperity you enjoy is based on how much revelation you are exposed to. This aligns with what God told Abraham, which was that all the land he could see would be given to him (Genesis 13:15). This meant that the only limitation to his possession was his revelation. In the Kingdom of God, we only advance to the extent of what has been revealed to us. This is why Apostle Paul prayed that the eyes of the Ephesian church be enlightened so that they may know *"what is the hope of His calling, and what is the riches of the glory of His inheritance in the saints."* (Ephesians 1:18)

In every corner of the globe, money is a universal symbol of prosperity, an emblem of success coveted by many. Yet, within the confines of the Church, a perplexing debate lingers: should we actively pursue prosperity as followers of Christ? It's a question that seems inconceivable to me. After all, can we truly envision a Heavenly Father who desires His beloved children to suffer in lack and deprivation? For some, the crux of the matter does not lie in whether God desires prosperity for His people but rather in the magnitude of that prosperity. It's akin to a classroom scenario where a dedicated teacher finds themselves instructing their own child. Would they not ardently desire their flesh and blood to soar above the rest, to excel rather than settle for mediocrity? Our Heavenly Father wants us to prosper (3 John 1:2), so He has made the information we need available to those interested.

A cornerstone represents a physical stone critical to a building's foundation and a fundamental element or principle. Think of it as the bedrock or a pillar upon which everything else stands. Historically, the cornerstone was often the first piece set in place during a building's construction, signifying its importance and foundational role. It's what everything else is built upon. So, in essence, the cornerstone is synonymous with the foundation itself.

Now, let's draw a parallel to our daily lives. Imagine surviving solely on desserts. However, as tempting as it may be to indulge in ice cream, cakes, and all sorts of sweets, they can only serve as the icing on the cake, so to speak. They are not the main course but an addition to what we've already consumed. This analogy brings us to the heart of our discussion on prosperity. When discussing prosperity, it's easy to get caught up in the "desserts" – the immediate gratifications and rewards. However, the cornerstone, or the foundation of true prosperity, often goes overlooked.

We hear repeatedly about the importance of giving – and indeed, giving is crucial. Yet, without a solid foundation, without adhering to certain fundamental principles, all the giving in the world may not lead us to the prosperity we seek. It raises the question: why do some give generously yet see no return? Is it possible that God's promises have failed? Absolutely not. The Scripture is clear: *"Let God be true, and every man a liar."* (Romans 3:4)

God's Word is infallible. So, if we find ourselves giving without receiving, it's time to reassess ourselves and our actions. It's not about giving alone but understanding and implementing the cornerstones of prosperity outlined in the scriptures. The passage in 2 Corinthians 9:6-11 offers profound insight into these fundamental principles of prosperity. Prosperity extends beyond mere monetary gains; it's the outcome of aligning our lives with God's truth.

I understand that the subject of prosperity can evoke strong emotions fraught with sensitivity for many. Yet, even as poverty serves as a stark reminder of perceived failure, we cannot reconcile ourselves to a theology that normalizes destitution and lack for believers. As we embark on this journey together, let us explore the profound implications of prosperity within the context of our faith, challenging preconceived notions and embracing a vision of abundance that aligns with the promises of our Heavenly Father. Abraham, Isaac, Jacob, and many other fathers of faith demonstrated that financial prosperity is something God gives, and we should look forward to learning how to walk in it. The essence of this book is to expose you to your financial inheritance in Christ and guide you in taking the right steps to actualize that financial inheritance.

1

The Cornerstones of Prosperity

The Bible is full of pathways for attaining the glorious destiny the Lord has ahead of us. One of such pathways available in scripture is for the acquisition of financial prosperity. In 2 Corinthians 9:6-11, we see the major keys for acquiring financial prosperity that extends beyond the sowing of financial seeds.

"But this I say: He who sows sparingly will also reap sparingly, and he who sows bountifully will also reap bountifully. So let each one give as he purposes in his heart, not grudgingly or of necessity; for God loves a cheerful giver. And God is able to make all grace abound toward you, that you, always having all sufficiency in all things, may have an abundance for every good work. As it is written: 'He has dispersed abroad, He has given to the poor; His righteousness endures forever.' Now may He who supplies seed to the sower, and bread for food, supply and multiply the seed you have sown and increase the fruits of your righteousness, while you are enriched in everything for all liberality, which causes thanksgiving through us to God." (2 Corinthians 9:6-11)

When we read scriptures like this, we must avoid the preconceived notion that financial prosperity can only materialize from sowing monetary seeds. Indeed, a significant part of prosperity relates to using money as a seed. However, we will be examining the full picture.

Cornerstone 1: The Essential Principle of Adding Value

This cornerstone involves maintaining an overwhelming desire to add value. I've heard testimonies from individuals who say they constantly remind themselves of the importance of value throughout their day. It is crucial because living without adding value is not truly living. Everything God created is meant to add value. Unfortunately, many people consume more than they produce, and this habit hinders prosperity. In the past, before the advent of money, trade was conducted through bartering, meaning that people had to produce something of value to exchange for what they wanted. Imagine if we still lived in such times and you produced nothing; you would receive nothing in return and owe others. Therefore, the first cornerstone of prosperity is to cultivate an overwhelming desire to add value, give, and be a blessing to others.

This overwhelming desire to be a blessing could manifest in giving those in need cars, houses, or scholarships. It can be a strong desire to care for orphans and the homeless. It starts with desire, even if the ability is not there yet. The Bible tells us that God provides seed to the sower (2 Corinthians 9:10). Those who have become blessings today will tell you that from the beginning, they were driven by a vision of how they could be a blessing, a passion so intense it often moved them deeply to begin to act on it. They prayed, "God, if You just bless me, I want to do this and that." The journey towards prosperity begins with an overwhelmingly strong desire to add value to others.

As you progress, let your desire to add value to others grow stronger and stronger. Let the number of people you want to be a blessing to continue to increase as the Lord blesses you. Your aspirations and desires should always exceed your current capabilities.

Cultivating and Acting on the Desire to be a Blessing

Many people lack the desire to give. When you ask some people about their financial aspirations, their answers revolve solely around themselves and their immediate family. This narrow vision does not reflect true prosperity. We must broaden our perspective and allow the needs of others to stir us into compassion far beyond what we think we can manage. Imagine encountering homeless individuals and praying, "God, bless me so I can build homes for them." Or meeting brilliant students who wish to pursue education but cannot do so because they cannot afford it. If you so choose, your prayer can become, "Lord, bless me so I can provide scholarships for those in need so that they can study without the burden of student loans." You might wonder, "But what if these desires never come to fruition?"

Remember, it all begins with the desire. The Bible assures us that God will fulfill the desires of our hearts, and it teaches us that love never fails. For example, Bill Gates is known to have donated billions of dollars every month to causes on continents he had never called home, such as Africa. The wealth that Bill Gates acquired is not inherited fortune but the result of his overwhelming desire to make a difference. He even inspired numerous other wealthy individuals to donate a huge chunk of their wealth before they passed away. Why wouldn't God bless someone with such intentions? Whether or not he identifies as a born-again Christian like you is irrelevant. The Bible is clear that *"The generous soul will be made rich, and he who waters will also be watered himself."* (Proverbs 11:25) If you have a strong desire to become an agent for adding value to others, the principles the Lord has established on the earth will ensure that you are empowered to add value.

Some Christians struggle with the idea of giving, even when it comes to giving to the house of God. Yet, they expect prosperity from God. I recall a conversation with a church member who expressed her wish to buy a house that year. That's a commendable goal and aligns with God's promises. She emphasized her desire to buy a house with a finished basement, which piqued my curiosity. Why was she so specific that it had to have a basement? She explained that she intended to provide temporary housing for new church attendees in Edmonton who couldn't afford rent, helping them stabilize their lives. 'It is already done,' I assured her. Some other people may want to buy a house only to flaunt it and capture the moment with a selfie on Facebook to impress others. Such motives stem from selfish desires, which do not align with God's purpose for us. God's blessings are not meant to feed our vanity but to enable us to be blessings to others.

Do you see yourself giving cars to people? It's not impossible. In fact, if a couple can give up private jets, what is a car in comparison? Some people cannot even envision themselves giving iPads or tablets to others. "Pastor, do you realize how much a tablet costs," you might ask. It is indeed possible. Harbour the desire, the intense longing to be a generational blessing. That is, "Lord, I aspire to be the one to purchase the church building when it's time for us to build." This desire is a personal matter between you and

God. You may ask, "What if it doesn't materialize?" Well, what if it does? This is where faith and desire converge. God provides seed to the sower, to those He recognizes as wanting to sow, not to those who merely consume, but to sowers. This is the first cornerstone of prosperity: to harbour an overwhelming desire to add value and be a blessing.

Resources for Adding Value: Time and Talent

There are two gifts bestowed upon everyone by God for prosperity: time and talent. If all a person does is consume entertainment, social media, food, movies, etc., but they are not producing anything, they will not prosper. Even dangerous givers who do not produce anything will not have room for housing God's blessings. The Bible makes it clear that whatever a person sows, they will reap (Galatians 6:7). The sowing here does not just refer to money. The sowing also refers to a mixture of time and talent. Your time and talent combined result in the value you add, which God will bless. This can be a business, a career endeavour, a social enterprise, etc. God's system for prosperity is for His children to give financially, and add value to Him, to authorities over their life, and to people in need while working diligently.

The identity of a believer that you carry should be the impetus for a passion to add value. Throughout your workday, there has to be something tangible that you have done to show that because you showed up to work that day, your workplace is better. Before you begin your work day, determine what value you will add. There is no way an organization can be going through financial challenges to the extent of needing to restructure, that they will say, 'You know what, we are restructuring so much that we do not need a CEO anymore.' It's impossible because they need the CEO position for the value he or she adds.

No matter how many people they let go in your organization, if you're adding value and God wants you to be there, nobody can move you, except if they don't know what they are doing. My wife shared with me that an organization she was familiar with was having a send-off party for an intern who only worked there for six months. That intern was so impactful that even the organization's CEO attended her send-off. So many people had wonderful things to say about how much value she had added within a short period of time. This contrasts with some of us who have been working for one year, two years, three years, or even ten years without focusing on adding value but waiting for retirement.

Dignity in Labour

A born-again believer should be the best worker any organization can have. If a believer works in an organization, their boss or coworkers must see the value they are adding. A lack of understanding of the need to add value can make some believers say they are not liked at work because of their spirituality. The reality could be that they are lazy or do not add value. Remember that Joseph and Daniel served unbelievers in Egypt and Babylon, respectively, yet they were highly honoured and valued in those environments. So, even though people knew they were religious, they could not be fired because they added value.

Our mindset should be, how am I adding value in this place, and how can I increase the value I am adding? There is dignity in work. I have heard people pray: 'God, give me lots of money but little work.' If that was how everybody was praying, who would do the work? Appreciate the dignity in your labour. Imagine Jesus' statement about working because His Heavenly Father is consistently working (John 5:17). What other work should the Creator of the universe do after all the work He has already done? This is evidence that there is dignity in labour. Enjoy the idea of work and the prospect of working one way or the other into your old age.

If only spiritually diligent believers could work as hard as they pray, they would turn the world upside down for good. There should not be a worldly person who is more diligent at work than a believer. Some people will say, "Oh yeah, Apostle, I would have worked hard, but it is just that because of all my church responsibilities and service attendance, I do not have more time to put into my secular work." Such people still finish watching many seasons of Netflix shows. Such people are still aware of everything happening in the Twitterverse (or perhaps Xverse) and keep a pulse of all trending. Where do they get the time to keep up with everything happening in their and other people's lives? Let's work and give; add value and prosperity will naturally and consistently flow in.

A while ago, the church contracted a church member to do some work. The amount was agreed upon, but when it was time to pay, the Holy Spirit said, "No, give him double for the work he did." I didn't ask why because I knew that he put in way more effort than was expected. Galatians 6:7 validates this truth. It is all about adding value and going above and beyond. God does not cheat people. Promotion happens when a person is already doing more work than the level they are currently at, and so they are moved higher. It's that simple.

Laziness does not have a place in the realm of prosperity and adding value. Even in spiritual matters, there is no place for lazy people because each one has to read the Word, fast, and pray. There's no future for someone who just wants to sit down and do nothing but wants the latest cell phone and car. Wake up, work, and love your work. The love might not come naturally but continue to tell yourself that you love your work until you finally do.

Cornerstone 2: Joyful Giving

Give joyfully at all times, in every instance, and in every place where there is an opportunity to give, to both God and humanity. I attended a believers' convention with Kenneth Copeland in Texas, and I had a profound experience in the hotel where the Holy Spirit spoke to me about this second cornerstone during my devotion, so I encourage you to pay close attention to this section.

I remember when my journey into prosperity began. I had heard various messages from preachers, but it wasn't until 2011 that I had an encounter with God on financial prosperity that I got understanding. In this encounter, I was walking and saw an old man carrying a Bible. Without hesitation, I approached him and offered to help carry it. As we walked, I noticed a man I didn't yet know personally, but he is known in Nigeria as a very wealthy man. I was so excited and exclaimed, "You attended my alma mater, the same school as me!" I couldn't stop smiling. Suddenly, he handed me a chequebook. I eagerly opened it, only to find that every page was signed, yet no amount was written. Confused, I woke up from the dream and asked the Lord for clarity. His response was profound: "I've given you a blank cheque." That was a prophecy. And so, my journey of prosperity began. Since then, and for a long time, most times when I closed my eyes to pray, I would receive instructions to give money to others. "Give twenty dollars. Give five hundred dollars. Give five thousand dollars. Give ten thousand." Many of us have encountered such divine instructions. The process continued, and I obeyed until one day when it stopped. Although I still give generously, those specific instructions stopped for that season, and that's when the tide turned, and blessings flowed abundantly.

The Essence of Giving

You can start by giving money. You may ask, 'How do I acquire money to give?' We earn money by utilizing our time by either offering a service or selling something. Thus, giving transcends monetary contributions. Giving can encompass your time or something of value to you. You might offer a service. For instance, we could hire a professional painter for perhaps $600 if the church required painting. However, if you are skilled in painting and decide to offer your services to God at no charge, that act is equivalent to donating $600 to the church. Such contributions are pleasing to God. Giving involves more than just money; it includes offering something of value to someone of value. This is crucial to understand, especially for those who may not have financial resources to give but possess skills and services that can bless others. Therefore, do not constrain yourself thinking, "I don't have money. I can only contribute if I have money." You possess skills that have monetary value that you can give to others. You can add value at all times, every time, and everywhere there is an opportunity. I am grateful to God for this grace that He has given to us.

Cultivating a Giving Mindset for Prosperity

The Bible teaches that it is more blessed to give than to receive (Acts 20:35). Adopting a mindset focused on assisting others ensures you will never lack prosperity. Conversely, a mindset fixated on what you can receive will invariably place you at a disadvantage. Someone gave an analogy: If you are always in the habit of asking for money, your hand will always remain underneath the giver's hand, and, hence, the giver will always be above you. Always think about giving. How can I give today? How can I be a blessing today? Giving is not just about money. It includes offering advice, counsel, inspiration, and motivation. The mentality of always receiving, receiving, receiving will foster a victim mentality, which is not the path to prosperity.

Always think about giving, starting from where you are. Don't overextend yourself when it comes to money unless you feel a specific prompting from God to offer a sacrifice. Do what you can, with what you have, where you are. Never let your situation prevent you from being a blessing. You might say, "Apostle, you don't understand my pain." Remember, everyone is always facing challenges. Don't let that stop you from blessing others in need. Rarely allow yourself to be in a position where you receive more than you give.

Focus on Adding Value

I have come to appreciate deeply and thank God that everyone has something valuable to offer others. I had the privilege of connecting with a minister of the Gospel whom God uses in remarkable ways. While he was having lunch with myself and other ministers, many only sought to get blessings from him, perhaps hoping for his hand to be laid on their heads. I looked for an opportunity to be of service to him. During our conversation, he mentioned a challenge he had been facing for some time—a challenge my wife and I have had the privilege of overcoming more than once. Recognizing this as a divine opportunity, I eagerly offered our assistance. "Sir, I want to help you with this," I said. He was very surprised. This shows that no matter anyone's status, there are always areas where they can use some support from others. It might not always be financial; sometimes, the most profound support comes in the form of dedicated prayers or fasting on their behalf—acts of service that don't need to be broadcasted but are seen and valued by God. This gesture of offering help without seeking anything in return left a lasting impression on him. In a world where many are focused on what they can receive, being remembered for what you give is powerful.

The Concept of Sowing and Reaping

Galatians 6 reminds us that God is not mocked: whatever a man sows, he will reap. This principle underscores the importance of giving or sowing into the lives of others. If we do not sow, we cannot expect to reap. The act of giving becomes not just a moral duty but a spiritual principle that guides our interactions and contributions to the lives of those around us.

I remember being in the ministry where we were at that time. I regularly paid my tithes and gave by God's grace at every meeting. But then, one day, while I was at work, I heard God tell me, "You should pay the church's rent for that month." It was not a small amount, so I thought, "No, that cannot be God." So, I continued working. Yet, the voice came again, saying, "You should pay the church's rent for that month." Then, I called the pastor to find out how much the rent was. When he told me, he asked, "Why are you asking?" I replied, "I just want to know." But the voice would not leave me. By the grace of God, I did it.

Many years after that, Cornerstone Christian Church of God was founded, and God told someone to pay the rent since we started. That person continued to pay the church's monthly rent for many years until I told the person to stop. Looking back, the total amount this person gave toward the church's rent was way more than what I was told to give to cover the rent of that church ministry. Some wonder, "Why don't people do things for me?" Perhaps it's because you are not being a blessing to others. *"God is not mocked"* (Galatians 6:7). If you're always looking for opportunities to sow, you will always be reaping.

CORNERSTONE 3: GIVE PURPOSEFULLY

Don't Give Emotionally

Don't allow your giving to be manipulated. Predetermine what you will sow, even before it is time. This principle is particularly important, especially in financial contributions to a church, servant of God, or other potentially emotional giving. I am grateful for the approach taken by our church, Cornerstone Christian Church of God. Offerings are prepared and collected during the announcement segment in a quick and pressure-free manner. There is no coercion to give, and there are no suggestions that failing to give will result in financial loss or other manipulative tactics. Such tactics do not reflect divine principles but rather resemble the fundraising strategies of secular organizations.

My wife and I have made it a practice to predetermine our contributions from home. Regardless of the emotional appeals or dramatic presentations during a service, we adhere to our predetermined offering unless we feel divinely inspired to adjust it. This approach aligns with the biblical principle that God loves a cheerful giver (2 Corinthians 9:7), emphasizing that offerings should be given freely, not under duress or manipulation. I know of instances in other ministries or organizations where individuals were condemned for not contributing. In a particularly troubling instance, congregants were even cursed for not giving to the church. This is a practice that is deeply unfortunate and regrettable. Giving should never be done under duress or coercion, as such contributions lack the blessings of voluntarily giving to God.

Giving to Those Who Add Value

Another aspect of purposeful giving is to give to people of value and who give you value. No farmer expecting to reap a harvest sows in an arid land. Those you give to should either hold value to you or be valuable to someone you care about, e.g. God. For your giving to result in financial prosperity, it must not be done for emotional reasons. It is not everyone in need that we are called to give to. An incident that took place with Jesus further illustrates this point.

"And being in Bethany at the house of Simon the leper, as He sat at the table, a woman came having an alabaster flask of very costly oil of spikenard. Then she broke the flask and poured it on His head. But there were some who were indignant among themselves, and said, "Why was this fragrant oil wasted? For it might have been sold for more than three hundred denarii and given to the poor." And they criticized her sharply. But Jesus said, "Let her alone. Why do you trouble her? She has done a good work for Me. For you have the poor with you always, and whenever you wish you may do them good; but Me you do not have always. She has done what she could. She has come beforehand to anoint My body for burial. Assuredly, I say to you, wherever this gospel is preached in the whole world, what this woman has done will also be told as a memorial to her." (Mark 14:3-9)

You must realize that for you to be blessed from your giving, it must not be given emotionally or as a result of someone manipulating you. The "poor" must not be the main group you give to if you want to rise. Purposeful giving involves you first giving to an anointing higher than you to rise. Who you give to is the one who has the power to increase you. Even when you eventually begin to give to the poor, understand that you are not giving to the poor but to the Lord (Proverbs 19:17).

Some people do what is right but at the wrong time. The principle is to give to those higher than you to be elevated. When you get up, you can begin to arrange to be a blessing to those below you. When I began my journey into financial prosperity, I ignored many needs of the "poor" and "needy" around me. I was sowing into those above me to lift me up so that I could eventually and sustainably be a blessing to people in need. You will likely become stranded financially if you attempt to start your journey into prosperity by giving to the poor.

Jesus made it clear that we will always have the poor with us. Not only that, the poor will always have needs. The poor will also have more poor friends who will come to you for their needs to be met. Focusing your attention on meeting the needs of the poor before you have access to unlimited resources is a financial death sentence. It is like driving on quicksand. It is like placing a heavy weight on the head of a 3-year-old child to carry. So Jesus endorsed the action of the woman who ignored all the "poor" people in Bethany to be a blessing to Jesus. She could be a blessing to the poor from the blessing she received from sowing into Jesus. Unfortunately, I have encountered many who got stranded financially because they ignored this vital principle. Some of those people have even become vindictive and cynical about Kingdom prosperity mainly because they did not see the results they were anticipating.

The Biblical Foundation for Voluntary Giving

In Exodus 35:4-5 we are told that God instructed Moses to collect an offering from the people to build the Tabernacle. Moses could have pressured the people, claiming God would punish them if they didn't contribute. Instead, Moses simply said to the congregation of Israel, "This is the thing which the Lord has commanded: Take from among you an offering to the Lord. Whoever is of a willing heart, let him bring it as an offering to the Lord: gold, silver, and bronze," among other things. After leaving Moses' presence, the entire assembly of the Israelites, those whose hearts were moved and spirits willing, contributed offerings for the construction of the Tabernacle.

Moses made the announcement, and the people gave willingly. Giving should always be between the individual and God without the need for it to be made public. At the end of the day, the results will show those who have given and those who have not. It's as simple as that.

"Then Moses called Bezalel and, Aholiab and every gifted artisan in whose heart the Lord had put wisdom, everyone whose heart was stirred, to come and do the work. And they received from Moses all the offering which the children of Israel had brought for the work of the service of making the sanctuary. So they continued bringing to him freewill offerings every morning. Then all the craftsmen who were doing all the work of the sanctuary came, each from the work he was doing, and they spoke to Moses, saying "The people bring much more than enough for the service of the work which the Lord commanded us to do." So Moses gave a commandment, and they caused it to be proclaimed throughout the camp, saying "Let neither man nor woman do any more work for the offering of the sanctuary." And the people were

restrained from bringing, for the material they had was sufficient for all the work to be done - indeed too much." (Exodus 36:2-7)

Cornerstone 4: Receive Thankfully

Be humble enough to receive from God, regardless of the vessel He uses to bless you. Many people follow steps one to three, but the fourth step is difficult. Some say, "No, me, I only give, I don't receive." However, this mindset hinders prosperity. The Bible states, *"Give, and it will be given to you: good measure, pressed down, shaken together, and running over will be put into your bosom. For with the same measure that you use, it will be measured back to you."* (Luke 6:38) God will cause men, women, young, and old to give to your bosom. He can use anyone to bless you, whether from your community, your ethnicity, or not, even someone of a different gender.

Be Humble Enough to Receive

It takes humility to receive from others. For instance, when you go to a restaurant and someone offers to pay for your meal, accept it graciously. Rejecting such gestures out of false pride is not holiness but rather arrogance. It is crucial to understand that receiving gifts from others is not a sign of weakness or dependency but a recognition of blessings. According to James 1:17, *"Every good gift and every perfect gift is from above, and comes down from the Father of lights, with whom there is no variation or shadow of turning."* Therefore, when people offer their help or gifts, whether cleaning your house or any other act of kindness, accept it with gratitude, understanding that it's an expression of love for God and goodwill. As the

Bible teaches, *"Whatever you did for one of the least of these brothers and sisters of mine, you did for me"* (Mattew 25:40 NIV). Thus, receiving with humility not only allows you to experience God's blessings but also enables you to bless others in return.

When people tell you: 'We can pay for someone to clean your home', or 'Oh, I just want to repair your car for free', or 'I just want to buy you coffee', receive it and say thank you. You don't need to argue. How will you be blessed if you don't receive blessings? It starts with little things sometimes. And then one day someone will buy you a car and you will just say "Oh wow, thank you very much, may God bless you richly". How simple is that? It doesn't mean you're a beggar or a pauper. It is wrong to think you are in need because you receive seeds and gifts from others. If you receive more than you give, you cannot prosper. If you consume more than you produce, you cannot prosper. So, the key is to give way more than we are receiving. To prosper, it is not just money we have to give. There is more to giving than money. A man's gift makes room for him (or a man's money, services, or value, etc.) And brings them before great men (Proverbs 18:16).

2

How to Identify Opportunities to Prosper

God wants all of His children to be prosperous. Prosperity means different things to different people. It's not just about money; prosperity also encompasses having good relationships and people you can count on and trust. Rich relationships are a form of prosperity, alongside financial abundance and the ability to pursue one's desires with money, particularly for good purposes. Excellent health is also considered prosperity because sickness can drain one's finances. Waking up with every part of your body working perfectly well signifies prosperity, as does having a sound mind and the ability to think properly, with a quick understanding of things.

WHAT ARE OPPORTUNITIES?

An opportunity is an event that God has created for us to prosper. It is a divine coincidence that God has put in place for us to prosper. It is when God ensures that a person is in the elevator at the right time to meet the person they need to meet. That's an opportunity. Ecclesiastes 9:11 says that *"the race is not to the swift, nor the battle to the strong, nor bread to the wise, nor riches to men of understanding, nor favor to men of skill, but time and chance happen to them all."* This is another definition of opportunity: when time and chance work in your favour. God gives His children their fair share of time and chance. The question is, do we make use of it? Time and chance happen to everybody. Meeting the right person at the right time could lead to a job opening without an interview. One can have all the gifts in the world, but if not given an opportunity to display that gift, it's a waste. May God give us opportunities, in Jesus' name.

Many people do not take advantage of opportunities because they do not come in the package we expect. We have imaginations, which is good, but sometimes, our imaginations can work against us if we are not careful. If God came like God and were easily accessible, He would no longer be God. God makes sure opportunities are wrapped in ways that people cannot see. He's not wicked, but He does that out of love so that His children connected to Him can see and pick up what other people cannot see. Some women would not have overcome the stiff competition that would have ensued if their husbands came in their full package. Some men might not have stood the chance of marrying the lady they are married to now if the whole package was visible to everybody from the onset. God made it that way so that other people would ignore that person until the person the Lord has appointed sees them. Remember that opportunities should be examined with the eyes of the spirit. Not all that glitters is gold. Likewise, not all that looks like trash is trash. Let the Lord open your eyes to see treasure hidden in trash.

Opportunities in Warfare

David

When David saw Goliath, he saw an opportunity. Opportunities can emerge in warfare, similar to David's encounter with Goliath. David's father, Jesse, told him to deliver food to his siblings at the battlefront with King Saul. That seemed like an ordinary errand, but this would give David the opportunity of a lifetime to face a giant in battle and be announced to the whole of Israel. The fact that opportunities are not always obvious highlights the importance of sensitivity in the face of unexpected opportunities.

"And David left his supplies in the hand of the supply keeper, ran to the army, and came and greeted his brothers. Then as he talked with them, there was the champion, the Philistine of Gath, Goliath by name, coming up from the armies of the Philistines; and he spoke according to the same words. So David heard them. And all the men of Israel, when they saw the man, fled from him and were dreadfully afraid. So the men of Israel said, 'Have you seen this man who has come up? Surely he has come up to defy Israel; and it shall be that the man who kills him the king will enrich with great riches, will give him his daughter, and give his father's house exemption from taxes in Israel.' Then David spoke to the men who stood by him, saying, 'What shall be done for the man who kills this Philistine and takes away the reproach from Israel? For who is this uncircumcised Philistine, that he should defy the armies of the living God?' And the people answered him in this manner, saying, 'So shall it be done for the man who kills him.' Now Eliab his oldest brother heard when he spoke to the men; and Eliab's anger was aroused against David, and he said, 'Why did you come down here? And with whom have you left those few

sheep in the wilderness? I know your pride and the insolence of your heart, for you have come down to see the battle.' And David said, 'What have I done now? Is there not a cause?' Then he turned from him toward another and said the same thing; and these people answered him as the first ones did. Now when the words which David spoke were heard, they reported them to Saul; and he sent for him. Then David said to Saul, 'Let no man's heart fail because of him; your servant will go and fight with this Philistine.'" (I Samuel 17:22-32)

This is an example of a classic opportunity: David got there ordinary and broke, but he left there enriched with great riches, exempt from taxes and married the king's daughter. Do you know what it was like to be married to the king's daughter in those times? There is a common saying that opportunity comes but once. There is some truth in that, but God is the One who controls time and seasons. If you've missed an opportunity and cry out to Him, He can recreate another opportunity for you. Therefore, in Jesus' mighty name, I declare that lost opportunities are restored back to you now.

Opportunities in Difficult Situations

Nehemiah

Another example of someone who made the best use of opportunities is Nehemiah.

"'O Lord, I pray, please let Your ear be attentive to the prayer of Your servant, and to the prayer of Your servants who desire to fear Your name; and let Your

servant prosper this day, I pray, and grant him mercy in the sight of this man.' For I was the king's cupbearer." (Nehemiah 1:11)

In Nehemiah 1, Nehemiah was a cupbearer. He saw the opportunity to complete the walls of Jerusalem. In the previous verses, he was sad when he heard that the walls of his hometown, the sacred city of Jerusalem, the holy city, were broken down. As a result of Nehemiah taking advantage of the opportunity presented to him to rebuild the walls of Jerusalem, his level had changed from being a cupbearer to a governor.

"Moreover, from the time that I was appointed to be their governor in the land of Judah." (Nehemiah 5:14)

Joseph

Another example is Joseph. He was an ordinary individual until an opportunity arose. The king had a dream and needed an interpretation. Not only did Joseph interpret the dream, he went above and beyond and told the King how he recommended that they solve the problem that would befall the land. They only brought Joseph in to interpret a dream, they didn't bring him in to provide a solution. Therefore, he could have just interpreted the dream and left. Instead, Joseph interpreted the King's dream and provided a solution to the problem presented in the dream.

After recommending the solution, he stepped back, but the king said: 'Who else can we get to do this but you?' Note that Joseph was a foreigner. In this day and age, we hear all sorts of things about inequality, sexism, racism, tribalism, and so on. When a person offers a well-considered solution to a problem, it can lead people to temporarily put aside their biases and focus on the merits of the idea. In these moments, the potential for progress can outweigh negative preconceptions about the source.

Economic Disruption

In Haggai 2:6, God says, *"I will shake Heaven and earth, the sea and dry land; and I will shake all nations."* When the famine happened in Egypt, and Joseph stepped in, it was a means for large amounts of money to be transferred from the people to the king, where all the land was now owned by the king. A lot of money was also transferred from Joseph's father, Jacob, a blessed man, to Egypt because of the famine. Every significant event in the world causes a transfer of wealth from one group of people to another. Sometimes, God Himself is the One stirring the pot to cause a transfer of wealth from unbelievers to believers.

"For thus says the Lord of hosts: 'Once more (it is a little while) I will shake Heaven and earth, the sea and dry land; and I will shake all nations, and they shall come to the Desire of All Nations, and I will fill this temple with glory,' says the Lord of hosts. 'The silver is Mine, and the gold is Mine,' says the Lord of hosts." (Haggai 2:6-8)

COVID-19

COVID was another opportunity for the earth to be shaken. Do you know that governments were not even negotiating the price of vaccines? In essence, anyone with a vaccine to sell could name their price. Unfortunately, many countries bought so many vaccines that they ended up destroying massive amounts of unused vaccines. It was a shaking of the earth, and it caused money to be moved from one place or group of people to another. So when God begins to speak about another earth-shaking moment, I just pause and ask, "Lord, in which direction should we move to take advantage of the shaking coming?"

Amidst events like the COVID-19 pandemic, Christians should consider what resources they can offer. Although the peak of the pandemic may have passed, its impact lingers. For instance, during COVID-19, prayer movements flourished as people sought solace in times of fear and uncertainty. As the world faces challenges like mental health issues at an alarming rate due to the pandemic and many other world crisis events, it's important for Christians not to panic like other people but to reflect on how we can contribute to solutions and seize financial opportunities as they arise.

Socio-Political Movements

There was a period when the Black Lives Matter movement took the world by storm, and protests were everywhere. It seems like the world has moved on from that now. Many people acted emotionally, and some even turned their properties black. Some people's lives will not remain the same because they wasted and destroyed things that should not have been destroyed. But underneath the belly of the whale, a lot was happening. Some people were getting wealthier and elevated due to the opportunities made possible by the protest. When a shaking happens, we must always ask ourselves what is happening behind the scenes. Don't let anything dissuade you from your journey to the top in life. You can bring about change when you get to the top, but climb to the top first. When you get there, use your platform to bring about change.

There was a time when movement towards diversity and inclusion was very pronounced. Due to this diversity movement, individuals who had never been considered for board or executive suite positions suddenly became the primary candidates. When the Bible talks about a shaking, it implies times of economic disruption, and there is no need to panic. Rather, we should recognize that this shaking could be the answer to prayers.

What do you think is happening when you hear that a country is giving another country military aid worth billions of dollars? All that is happening is that money is moving to those who control the defence industrial complex and make the weapons of war. Do you realize that for every announcement of billions of dollars in aid to Israel, Ukraine, etc., those who own the defence industries are getting richer? The government does not necessarily give equipment to those countries. Instead, the government is placing an order with the defence companies while footing the bill.

By providing solutions, individuals can benefit financially, bless others, and reinvest in the community. In times of panic, people are more inclined to make impulsive decisions without negotiation. Think about a woman in heavy labour who is very thirsty. She will most likely buy any water she sees without fighting over the price. People who panic are focused on immediate relief. Recognizing opportunities and responding with solutions can lead to mutually beneficial outcomes for everyone involved.

Opportunities in Change

The world has and will continue to experience changes. The extent and potential impact of the change can range from an evolution to a revolution. One such change is the advent of artificial intelligence (AI). The earlier you can ride on a revolutionary change, the better your chances of connecting to generational and monumental wealth. If you are unaware, you must realize that AI is here to stay. AI has and will continue to permeate many aspects of our lives. AI will change almost every industry in unrecognizable ways. Instead of seeing AI as a sign of the end of the world, why not see it as a tool to fulfill your life's purpose?

Parents, please do not encourage your children to study school courses that are no longer relevant. You do not want your children to graduate with loads of student loans and still not get a job because AI tools have taken over what they studied. As of February 2024, Tyler Perry shelved plans for his studio's multimillion-dollar expansion after seeing a demo of what OpenAI's Sora model can do. If OpenAI's ChatGPT, Google's Gemini, etc., are currently impressing the world today with their capabilities, how advanced do you think those programs will be after you graduate from your program in 4 years?

Examine the prospects of your program of study in light of AI advancement. The prognosis is so serious that many experts are recommending that governments prepare to give universal basic income (UBI) to their citizens because at least 40% of current jobs will be entirely taken over by AI. When the Holy Spirit leads you to a program, expect to succeed in it. The Holy Spirit knows what will come about tomorrow and has considered both your and the world's past, present, and future.

Partnership with the Holy Spirit

There was a particular officer in the Book of Second Kings (2 Kings 7:1-2) when there was a famine in the land in the days of Elisha. Elisha went to the king and prophesied that the famine would have ended by tomorrow. This officer replied that even if God were to open the windows of Heaven, the financial abundance Elisha predicted could not happen. Now, imagine that man was wise. If this man had been wise, he would have bought food and other items at low prices in anticipation of the price increase.

This happens when we have partnered with the Spirit of God for wealth generation, which will be discussed later in this book.

Partnership puts us in a position where God shows us the next wave of wealth transfer. He might not tell you everything He's doing, but He'll begin to direct you on the right path. Go and study this program. Go and take this course. Go and do this. Go and do that. He might not tell you that the time is coming when this skill will be extremely valuable. He might not tell you that, but you are following the Holy Spirit's instructions because you are confident in your partnership. Do not follow trends, follow the Holy Spirit. Trends are based on past information. There was a time when people were advised to study nursing, but those who saw the opportunity ahead of time and stepped in made more than most people. After a while, we began to hear that there was money in Information Technology. Now, the money has moved to Artificial Intelligence. The job of the Holy Spirit is to prepare us ahead of time for these opportunities.

As we partner with the Holy Ghost, let him begin to direct you. Instructions are one thing, but direction is another thing. I understand direction as a combination of several instructions. This is where the Holy Spirit will say, "Okay, now let's go in this direction, let's go down this path." A member of CCCG, when he was done with his undergraduate program, had pressure from his family to take up another program. He asked me for direction, and through inspiration by the Holy Spirit, I said, "That's a waste of time. Stay in what you're doing now. Because this is your future."

Popular gospel instrumentalist Dappy T. Keys is a career professional but followed the instruction of the Holy Spirit to stay in music. As of writing this book, his YouTube channel is currently the number 1 Christian piano instrumental channel on YouTube, with over 1 million subscribers and more than 300 million views. Imagine if he had ignored the Holy Spirit and focused on his career. The Holy Spirit knew that a time would come when people would need calm music because of the series of chaotic events that the world would experience. I cannot remember how many people I have personally told about his music. Stay where God leads you, and stop chasing shadows. It takes faith, discipline, and consistency to run with what the Lord tells you to do, especially when it doesn't look like it.

3

How to Take Advantage of Opportunities

There was a very dire situation portrayed in 2 Kings 6:26-31. The king became angry and desired to seize the head of Elisha, a prophet in the land. In the subsequent chapter, Chapter 7, in verse one, Elisha proclaimed, *"Hear the word of the Lord. Thus says the Lord, tomorrow about this time, a seah of fine flour shall be sold for a shekel, and two seahs of barley for a shekel, at the gate of Samaria."* Now, let's imagine Joseph in this situation. Imagine what he would have done after hearing about the impending prosperity and recognizing Elisha as a true prophet of God. He would have likely been acquiring properties and preparing for the coming abundance.

I read a few years ago that during the heat of the 2008 Subprime Mortgage Crisis, some homes in the U.S. were being foreclosed and sold by banks for as little as one dollar. I believe some people took advantage of that opportunity. No matter how damaged the houses were, even the land would have cost way more than $1. People often miss opportunities because they do not arrive in the package they expected. Here are some nuggets for taking advantage of opportunities.

KEEP THE FAITH

As believers, our faith is grounded in the assurance that God works all things together for our good. This foundational truth, rooted in Romans 8:28, is a beacon of hope and reassurance amid life's trials and tribulations. Regardless of how challenging a situation may be, we can rest in knowing that God orchestrates every circumstance for our benefit. Consider the story of Joseph in the Old Testament. Despite being sold into slavery by his own brothers and enduring years of hardship and injustice, Joseph remained steadfast in his faith and obedience to God. In the end, God used Joseph's trials to position him for greatness, ultimately elevating him to a position of authority in Egypt and orchestrating the reconciliation of his family.

Similarly, in modern times, we encounter countless testimonies of God's faithfulness in adversity. Take, for example, the story of a couple in Nigeria who were expecting a child while living in poor circumstances. When the wife unexpectedly gave birth to quintuplets, their situation seemed very overwhelming. Yet, through their unwavering faith and trust in God's providence, their story testified to His miraculous provision. In their hardship, God orchestrated a divine intervention by touching the heart of a Christian official who extended a generous hand of assistance. The couple experienced a remarkable turnaround, receiving a free house and employment opportunities that transformed their lives.

Indeed, the essence of Romans 8:28 lies not merely in the belief that God can turn any situation around for our good but in the unwavering faith to trust in His sovereignty and providence. Faith empowers us to view every circumstance through the lens of opportunity, recognizing that even the most challenging trials can serve as catalysts for divine blessings and breakthroughs. As we meditate on the truth of Romans 8:28, let us cultivate a mindset of faith and expectancy, knowing that God is continually at work in our lives, orchestrating every detail for our benefit. In every setback, disappointment, or adversity, let us declare with confidence that all things work together for our good, which will position us for divine opportunities and prosperity beyond measure.

Do Not Complain

Complaining is far from a harmless expression of frustration and has profound spiritual implications. It not only hinders the move of God but also reflects a lack of faith in His sovereignty and goodness. The Israelites in the wilderness serve as a poignant example of the destructive nature of complaining. Despite God's miraculous deliverance from slavery in Egypt, they grumbled and murmured against Him, resulting in dire consequences and prolonged wandering in the desert. In our own lives, complaining often serves as a barrier to experiencing God's blessings and breakthroughs. When we focus on our grievances and shortcomings, we magnify the negative aspects of our circumstances, blinding ourselves to the opportunities and blessings that God may provide amidst the challenges.

Instead of complaining, we are called to adopt an attitude of gratitude and thanksgiving. Regardless of the severity of our trials, we can choose to thank God for His faithfulness and provision, trusting that He is working all things together for our good. Even in the face of adversity, our decision to give thanks becomes a powerful declaration of faith in God's ability to redeem and restore every situation. Developing a habit of thanksgiving at all times is key to overcoming the temptation to complain. By cultivating a heart of gratitude, we shift our focus from our problems to God's promises, opening our eyes to the opportunities and blessings surrounding us. Thanksgiving is the antidote to complaining, transforming our perspective from pessimism to optimism, from blame to appreciation.

Moreover, giving thanks in times of delay, loss, and pain is a profound act of faith. It signifies our trust in God's ability to turn even the most challenging circumstances into opportunities for growth and blessing. Rather than dwelling on the negatives, we anchor our hope in God's unfailing love and provision, confident that He will fulfill His promises in His perfect timing. In essence, complaining robs us of the joy, peace, and blessings that accompany a life of faith and gratitude. By embracing a spirit of thanksgiving and trust in God's sovereignty, we position ourselves to receive His abundant blessings and recognize the opportunities for prosperity He places before us. Therefore, let us cast off the shackles of complaining and embrace the freedom and abundance in a heart overflowing with gratitude and praise. The Bible tells us that joy is essential if we draw from the wells of salvation (Isaiah 12:3). Without joy, we cannot draw inspiration from the Holy Spirit, which means that a believer can become stuck in an unpleasant situation. Do not allow anything to steal your joy.

Pay Attention to Others' Complaints

People's complaints are just coded ways of telling you they need help. And it is God's way of showing you the opportunities in a place. You should not complain but listen to other people's complaints. Before transitioning into full-time ministry, I worked as a business consultant in one of the "Big Four" consulting companies. We were taught in consulting to listen to the issues clients complained about and take note of them. Those client complaints, known as pain points, were future business opportunities in disguise. Do you want to be a world changer? Train yourself to hear and understand what other people complain about. Synthesize their complaints into areas that tie into your assignment and keep track of them. While in consulting, we used to ask questions like, "What are your pain points? What are the issues you are having?" In essence, "Complain, to my hearing." When you hear people complaining that they have back pains and body aches, for example, they might say that they need a solution, perhaps a massage. Listen to people's complaints because therein lie opportunities. It's a coded message from God to you. Even hearing your enemies' complaints can provide a significant battle advantage.

Gideon saw the opportunity to move in to fight, and he took the opportunity.

"It happened on the same night that the Lord said to him, 'Arise, go down against the camp, for I have delivered it into your hand. But if you are afraid to go down, go down to the camp with Purah your servant, and you shall hear what they say; and afterward your hands shall be strengthened to go down against the camp.' Then he went down with Purah his servant to the outpost of the armed men who were in the camp. Now the Midianites and Amalekites, all the people of the East, were lying in the valley as numerous as locusts; and their camels were without number, as the sand by the seashore in multitude. And when Gideon had come, there was a man telling a dream to his companion. He said, 'I have had a dream: To my surprise, a loaf of barley bread tumbled into the camp of Midian; it came to a tent and struck it so that it fell and overturned, and the tent collapsed.' Then his companion answered and said, 'This is nothing else but the sword of Gideon the son of

Joash, a man of Israel! Into his hand God has delivered Midian and the whole camp.' And so it was, when Gideon heard the telling of the dream and its interpretation, that he worshiped. He returned to the camp of Israel, and said, 'Arise, for the Lord has delivered the camp of Midian into your hand.'" (Judges 7:9-15)

How can you get promoted? Simply listen to what your boss is complaining about. What are they complaining about? Are they complaining about other people, other members of staff, your colleagues, or a situation at the office? And if you're able to address it, then do so. That doesn't mean you're sucking up to them. No, it is wisdom. So pay attention to what people are complaining about. It is an indirect message from God to you. I heard the story of two gentlemen waiting for a transportation bus to go home in a particular African country. They waited for a long time, and there were no bus scheduling systems then. One of the men kept complaining and was just angry, but the other man saw an opportunity. Instead of complaining, he thought, "Wow, this is an opportunity. Look at so many people waiting for buses. I can buy a bus and get a driver to plow this route. There will be lots of customers." So, one person saw problems and challenges and complained, while the other saw opportunities.

God has given everybody an equal share of opportunities because He's no respecter of persons. Once you identify what people are complaining about, ask God and seek how to solve those problems. Once you find solutions, you are on a journey to prosperity. Today almost many of us have access to different Bible translations simultaneously through tablets and other mobile devices. It's an opportunity that someone saw to make the Bible translations more accessible. Some people may have thought, "Oh, who needs tablets? Everybody has a laptop." But there was a need.

Provide a solution to the problem people complain about as quickly as possible because you're likely not the only one seeing the opportunity. The moment you see it, seize the opportunity immediately. If the Holy Spirit says no, then that's an exception. Do not fall into analysis paralysis by continuously going over the opportunity. If you are filled with the Holy Spirit, born again, and not feeling uncomfortable about the idea, jump on it immediately.

Jesse Duplantis shared a mind-blowing story of an occurrence many years ago. He said his friend came to him and said, *"Hey, there's a piece of land we can buy together. It costs three thousand dollars."* According to the story, he had a thousand dollars with him, and his friend suggested that they pull in a third friend, and they could all contribute a thousand dollars each and own the land together. Jesse Duplantis said, "Oh, I have to confirm if this is God." And he had the money. Why would God talk to you when you already have the money, and it is not a big deal for you? After much back and forth, Jesse Duplantis finally decided not to proceed with the deal. Remember that the Holy Spirit is not confused and will not go back and forth with us. The Holy Spirit will give clear instructions. A few weeks or months later, the government decided that a bridge would go over that piece of land, and the government bought that piece of land from that man for three million USD. What a profit! May you not lose any opportunity again in Jesus' name.

An opportunity is God's way of repaying you and me by blessing us. Be sensitive to opportunities. Listen to what people are complaining about. You might hear mothers complaining: "We need to work, and finding someone to take care of our children is challenging. We can pay any amount if we find someone, especially if they are Christian." That is God telling you to open your ears and listen. The bigger and the more problems you solve, the higher you go because the more problems you solve, the more value you create. The more value you create from the problems you solve, the more blessings and prosperity you attract. Every successful organization is solving a problem that people have. A car wash is solving the problem of dirty cars. Doctors are solving the problem of sick people. Counsellors are solving the problem of people with emotional or relational needs. With fast delivery, Amazon is solving the problem of people wanting to buy things from anywhere as cheaply as possible. Be a solution and prosperity will always be where you are.

4

How to Escape Poverty

Proverbs 22:2 highlights a fundamental truth: *"The rich and the poor have this in common: the Lord is the maker of them all."* This profound statement underscores the only shared attribute between the rich and the poor. Beyond this connection of sharing the same Creator, God, their experiences are as different as night and day. This realization brings us to an important insight: escaping poverty requires a radical change in mindset.

Consider the scenario where both a rich person and a poor person receive a million dollars. Their reactions would likely be drastically different. The poor person might have wasted money before hastily distributing their newly found wealth among family and friends, driven by guilt over their abundance. This act of emotional and sentimental generosity causes them to waste their wealth, leaving them with only a fraction of the original amount. This is exactly how a mindset of scarcity and guilt can pull one back into poverty, no matter how much wealth is gained.

Tyler Perry's journey provides a tangible example of this principle. When he started earning significant amounts of money, he would give it all away, ending each year broke. This pattern of misplaced generosity, rooted in the guilt of having so much more than those around him, led to a cycle of financial instability. It took him years to recognize that this fate was influenced by a poverty mentality. He realized that feeling guilty for having more than others prevented him from maintaining and growing his wealth. We must let go of so many thought patterns and habits to escape poverty.

THE HABIT OF LAZINESS

A habit of laziness is a habit of wasting time or, as some people will say, killing time. A lazy person is comfortable watching time pass by. You know, our life is made up of blocks of time. The other extreme of not doing anything is being anxious or in haste, which is not good either. Both extremes can result in wasting time. Some are always anxious and in haste but still end up nowhere. Those who allow anxiety into their hearts are just hurrying up, always busy-looking, spinning their wheels, yet going nowhere. A lazy person is simply destroying their lives with their own hands. Here is a picture of how dire it is for a lazy person. A lazy person has a field that is not utilized, hence the decadence that they experience.

"I went by the field of the lazy man, And by the vineyard of the man devoid of understanding; And there it was, all overgrown with thorns; Its surface was covered with nettles; Its stone wall was broken down. When I saw it, I considered it well; I looked on it and received instruction: A little sleep, a little slumber, A little folding of the hands to rest; So shall your poverty come like a prowler, And your need like an armed man." (Proverbs 24:30-34)

Your field is your assignment, whether you are called to be a nurse, doctor, accountant, IT professional, teacher, or minister. That is the work that

Jesus has given you, and it is important to be prudent and backed with all the information we need to succeed. I heard a leading minister say that some people in ministry don't understand the full essence of their ministry. They get a calling from God to begin ministry and immediately start a church, lacking the information they need and full of ignorance and assumptions. If God calls a person into the IT industry, they can choose to believe that being in IT just has to do with repairing computers because they didn't take the time to study and ask questions.

The field of a lazy man is full of thorns because their minds are so full of unprocessed ideas; books that have not been written, businesses that have not been started, or even songs that have not been released. Another scripture says a slothful person does not roast what he caught in hunting (Proverbs 12:27). A lazy person went to the field to hunt, brought the meat and the carcass home, but did nothing to it. They keep saying, 'I'll do it tomorrow.' It's like buying food that should be stored properly to avoid it going bad, and they leave the food on the counter, in the bag that it came with from the store. The food will eventually go bad, and money will be wasted.

How To Break the Habit of Laziness

Ensure you see things through. Don't just rejoice at the beginning of an assignment. Praise God when you start things, but don't end there. Let your anticipation grow. The Bible says about Jesus, *"...who for the joy that was set before Him endured the cross, despising the shame, and has sat down at the right hand of the throne of God."* (Hebrews 12:2) If you rejoice in the beginning as if you have already reached the end, you might not be encouraged to push through to the actual end. So, we thank Jesus for the beginning. We thank Him and anticipate the thanksgiving you will give Him at the end. These days, people celebrate the opening of a business as if they have made a million dollars already. Don't get me wrong, thanksgiving is good, but don't leave things at that.

The Role Your Environment Plays

Whoever taught us not to be diligent and to be lazy has taught us to be poor. There are nations with tourist attractions where people travel long distances to rest. One common thing among these places is that many of the residents are not very wealthy, even though many travel distances to spend lots of money there. Many residents of those nations try to imitate the tourists and are not diligent in accumulating wealth. These tourists look to relax after working hard, leaving the residents to learn the art of relaxation. The residents rarely see the hard work behind the scenes, only the laid-back holiday vibe the tourists bring. This can lead to a culture where the money flows out as easily as it flows in.

If a person is just getting started in their journey or accumulating wealth and they try to imitate those who have been consistent and established, that person will not last. That's the truth. We must ensure we are not copying the principles they are following now at the level they have gotten to. We look at what they did when they were starting and follow that. There's a time to fast aggressively because you are building spiritual power. Then, there's a time to read aggressively. There's a time to focus more on authority because you need to sustain and build an organization. Let's not fall into laziness by ignoring principles and not intentionally be lazy because it can stimulate poverty.

If you grew up in a place where laziness is practically a cultural heritage and time seems like a concept from a sci-fi novel, this might sound familiar. Imagine a place where the daily routine consists of waking up, strolling outside, and just sitting. It's a family affair: grandpa's out there, dad's joining in, and they're all teaching the youngsters the fine art of sitting and passively observing the world. From dawn to dusk, they're champions of lack of productivity, experts in the art of doing absolutely nothing but enjoying fresh air.

So, here's the deal: the whole culture of "resting" needs a rethink. What's the point of resting if you haven't done anything to rest from? While it's fine for tourists to relax, locals should have a different game plan rather than possibly napping their way to the bottom. Let's flip that script. Say goodbye to endless snoozing and hello to earning your rest. Agreeing to this might feel weird—like, "Am I really saying 'amen' to less sleep?" Think about it: there's nothing sweeter than getting into bed after a day packed with accomplishments. I often joke about starting a new trend where beds only appear when the individual has earned it. Imagine that— the doorbell rings, "Surprise! You worked hard. Here's your bed back." That's a motivation to get up and do something, right?

A Stingy Mindset

Whoever taught you to be stingy has taught you to embrace poverty. There are some homes where giving is considered a capital offence. If they hear you give to God, it's almost as if you have committed murder. Receiving is, of course, welcomed. But giving? "Oh my goodness, we don't have enough," they say. They bring up one person with a problem, another with a bigger problem, and another, and another, and question your decision to give. That's a mindset of poverty. Think about nations that only receive and never give back. They receive aid from everywhere. Yet, you ask yourself, with all the aid they've been receiving, have they come out of poverty? Receiving aid without giving back only entrenches poverty rather than alleviating it. Therefore, we need to change this mindset. This is why Jesus held the widow in high esteem. Despite her lack, she still gave. When Elijah encountered the widow of Zarephath, he had to correct her mindset first. He said, "Go and make for me first," because he could not bring abundance into a poverty mentality. That mindset cannot make money multiply. Wealthy people look for opportunities to be a blessing. The Bible says in 2 Corinthians 9:6, *"But I say this: He who sows sparingly will also reap sparingly, and he who sows bountifully will also reap bountifully."* Growing up, I observed many instances where people brought their offerings squeezed tightly in their hands before being dropped in the collection plate, reflecting the least effort and dignity in giving. This is an example of giving sparingly.

The Holy Spirit asked me a question I would like to ask you: "Would you encourage or discourage monumental acts of faith and giving?" If you were Solomon's father and he wanted to give a thousand burnt offerings, would you encourage him? What would your response be if you were the Heavenly Father, and your Son wanted to sacrifice Himself for the world? If you were a friend or relative of Abraham and he shared his intention to sacrifice Isaac, would you support or challenge him? The reality is that most people with a poverty mentality would likely discourage such acts. This mentality of discouraging giving hinders prosperity.

As prosperous individuals, we must embrace generosity, which stems from an abundance mindset. This principle was evident when our church building needed renovations, and we faced a financial dilemma with the contractor. God instructed us to sow what seemed insufficient into another ministry undergoing a similar project. At that time, $5,000 was as valuable as gold, given our financial commitments and the cost of renovations, and so being asked by God to sow that into another ministry was a huge act of faith. This decision to obey reflected a mindset of generosity and faith, demonstrating that giving is integral to prosperity. It is not enough to claim we are not stingy; we must show it through our actions. That generosity led to abundant financial provision running into hundreds of thousands of dollars from various nations.

Growing up, my family instilled in us the value of giving over receiving. My parents would distribute food to others or even sometimes decline our requests for money for unnecessary things so they could be a blessing to others. They also taught us to allocate a portion of our money for our offerings to God. Through these experiences, we learned the value of generosity, a lesson that has stayed with us and led us on a path to prosperity.

A WASTEFUL LIFE

A life of waste will lead to poverty. The more waste there is, the more likely a person will end up in poverty and penury. The habit of wasting resources and laziness squanders time and energy. However, this wastefulness extends beyond merely squandering time and energy; it also includes wasting food, money, and other resources. Some individuals waste intentionally, while others do so unintentionally, often due to laziness.

I once watched a documentary featuring a multi-billionaire from one of the royal families in the UAE. He spoke about his extensive business holdings across the globe, spanning nearly every nation. During the documentary, he led the interviewers to a room filled with flags representing each country where he had investments all around the table. The interviewer posed a particularly insightful question: "When do you sleep?" Determining an optimal sleep schedule posed a challenge considering the diverse time zones of his investments. The billionaire explained that he typically slept from 10 a.m. to 2 p.m. This schedule allows him to be active during the prime working hours of most countries, maximizing his ability to oversee his investments effectively. It's easy to declare by faith: "I'm a multi-billionaire", but do you know the work involved in managing businesses worth multi-billion? This means that waste cannot be something we play around with, and the discipline of management must be imbibed to avoid it.

Knowing how resources come but not how they are used up is a wasteful habit that cannot lead to prosperity. Even givers should track their giving. Jesus told the disciples after He multiplied five loaves and two fishes to gather the fragments. So, as people rejoiced at the food multiplying, Jesus was conscious of the fragments. Gather the fragments in your resources, and make sure the fragments don't go to waste. Someone testified at CCCG and said that she looked around her house to gather up all the money and found eight hundred dollars! Some people have been sent cheques that they perhaps forgot to cash or left cash in an envelope they forgot about. Gather up the fragments, God never blesses wasters.

It will shock you that the richer a person is, the more judicious they are of their resources. Those who are truly wealthy, whose assets are more than liabilities, do not waste food as much as people who are not wealthy. The issue of waste is very critical in the school of prosperity. It is so much so that when Jesus multiplied the five loaves and two fishes, He watched for the waste. We must be careful to plug holes that facilitate waste and put the right systems in place. In some homes, the mindset is, "Let us eat and drink today, for tomorrow we die," so they go on vacations with money they don't have, accumulate credit card debt, and then pay interest on money they did not have to spend. That's waste. If you need to take some time off and cannot afford to travel, go on a stroll, visit a friend in town, or do something different from your regular routine. These are cheaper ways to rest. Many people go on vacations, and the thrill only lasts a few days upon return. That is not worth spending money that you don't have.

A Borrowing Habit

To remain on a path to prosperity, never make borrowing your first option. When you need something, the first thing that comes to mind shouldn't be, "Who can I borrow it from so I can pay it back?" We know that the value of money fluctuates. The money you borrowed from someone a year ago isn't worth the same today because it can only buy fewer things. Yes, you're repaying the same amount, but in terms of the value of the money, you're actually repaying more. The rich often have power over the poor, and the borrower is a servant to the lender (Proverbs 22:7). If you are always so quick to borrow, you do not give yourself a chance to consider if you could have obtained what you want for free. Some things could have been given to us as gifts, but instead, we chose to borrow, so they were lent to us.

I understand that unfortunately, some people might be depending on their credit cards. Now if this is you, may God help you get out of that situation in the name of Jesus. Not everyone needs to depend on their credit card because a credit card does not represent a person's money. I trust the Lord that we'll reach a point where the cars and homes we purchase, will be obtained without a mortgage by the special grace of God. Nobody will criticize you for believing that. Some of us come from countries where mortgages aren't common, where people fully own their houses. Sometimes, we can become so indoctrinated into an environment and system that we believe there's no other way to acquire things without debt.

The habit of borrowing solidifies poverty. Don't be quick to become a person who always asks friends, "Hey, can you quickly lend me a hundred dollars?" No, instead of that, try, "Hey, do you have some change you can spare?", "Hey, I need 50 bucks. Can you help me out?" You're talking to a friend, not begging. Don't be quick to borrow money. Borrowing not only causes poverty, it also damages relationships. Let borrowing always be the last option after you've explored all other avenues. Proverbs 22:7 tells us, *"The rich rule over the poor, and the borrower is servant to the lender."* Isn't it interesting how poor folks often borrow on unfavorable terms? They hardly get to negotiate. But when a rich person needs to borrow, suddenly, the terms are all in their favour. Why? Well, because they've got the upper hand.

I was watching this documentary about how the wealthy can afford fancy things like yachts. They stash money in trusts, and the trust handles the purchase. Sometimes, they can even obtain loans at 0% interest and pay nothing upfront. Meanwhile, regular people end up with credit card debts and pay interest over 20%. Let's face it, money can be a sensitive topic. There are things we have convinced ourselves we cannot live without. It's sad to see families drowning in debt, with everyone owing everyone else. Shedding light on issues like these is a big step to breaking such demonic cycles. Even if you are currently unable to live without your credit card, you can still believe that you do not need it and that one day, you will do without it. Never make excuses for a temporary situation and mistakenly make it permanent.

Making Pledges

A pledge means standing as a guarantor, signifying that if the primary person fails to pay, the one making the pledge will take on the responsibility. This concept is discussed in Proverbs 22:26-27, written by Solomon, one of the wealthiest individuals in history. *"Do not be one of those who shakes hands in a pledge, one of those who is surety for debts; If you have nothing with which to pay, Why should he take away your bed from under you?"* (Proverbs 22:26-27) Solomon warns against becoming ensnared in financial agreements that require pledging, emphasizing the potential pitfalls of hastily co-signing for others. Being a surety for someone else's debts can lead to unforeseen consequences, especially if the guarantor lacks the means to fulfill the obligation. A pledge is simply you saying to a lender, "If the borrower cannot pay, hold me responsible for the loan." If you are not confident of the person's ability to repay a loan, do not make the mistake of co-signing a loan with them.

Do not make emotional decisions about your financial security. The consequences of making emotional financial decisions can be severe. It is better to offend a friend or family member and protect your financial future than to destroy your financial security because you want to please a relative or close friend. Poverty often thrives in a communal mindset, where individuals may feel obligated to assist others despite their personal financial constraints. Even with good intentions, co-signing for someone else's debt carries significant risks. A single default by the borrower can have severe repercussions for the co-signer, potentially resulting in the loss of personal assets. If you have put yourself in a compromising position already, pray and ask the Lord to rescue you before it is too late.

AN AVERAGE MINDSET

The life of being average is one of doing the barest minimum. An average person is not lazy, but they're also not diligent. They just do enough so that nobody will say they didn't do anything. We must ensure that we don't do only what we are told to do but much more. We must always seek to do something extra; make it a habit. It's one of the traits of highly blessed and prosperous people. Always go the extra mile.

As mentioned earlier in Chapter 2, Joseph was called to interpret dreams. He wasn't called to bring solutions. But after interpreting the dream, Joseph decided to go the extra mile. Joseph gave Pharaoh something extra. From today, make a decision not to hoard value. Go above and beyond. Someone asked you to go help them buy a shirt, for example, and you know it's meant to be a gift for someone else. You can also decide to get a gift bag. Even if the person who sent you on the errand did not need a gift bag, your actions show that you have initiative and can be trusted with bigger things. Amazon is where it is today because it always chooses to go the extra mile for its customers. The culture at Amazon is that the customer is king.

Sometimes, individuals do not take this proactive approach of going above and beyond if it is not requested for fear of giving away too much for free. This is also a scarcity mindset. When someone else presents an idea, an individual responding with a dismissive "Yeah, I know, it came to my mind" reflects poorly on that individual's initiative. Imagine if everyone approached their work with the mindset of continually seeking opportunities to contribute and improve. The potential within every human being is so vast, yet some settle for mediocrity due to a reluctance to invest extra effort. Recognizing opportunities for improvement but choosing to ignore them out of a perceived burden of extra work only perpetuates a cycle of averageness.

I once wondered why some vehicles are very expensive. When you look at the Rolls Royce and how it is made, you understand why it is costly. There's nothing average about it. The things that you would not even think anybody should pay attention to, they pay attention to. Going the extra mile will take us away from the level of being average. Whoever taught you to be average has taught you to be poor. *"Do you see a man who excels in his work? He will stand before kings; He will not stand before unknown men."* (Proverbs 22:29)

EXCEED EXPECTATIONS

It is essential to break free from complacency and embrace a continuous improvement mindset. Even when tasks seem mundane, approaching them with enthusiasm and a willingness to go above and beyond can yield significant results. Let's challenge ourselves to exceed expectations and contribute wholeheartedly to our shared goals. No matter the level, there's something better to achieve.

There are some families where staying back an extra hour or so at work or church is frowned upon and seen as a problem mainly because diligence is not understood in those homes. In such homes, perhaps, staying an extra hour to chill at a friend's house is considered normal. The Bible says if you cannot manage what is another man's, who will give you your own? When properly managed, the mindset of going the extra mile can be a key to success. Think about it: nobody can pay you what you're truly worth. That's why always striving to do more than what you are paid for is crucial. *As stated in the book Think and Grow Rich, it's like raising your salary.* Your aim should always be to exceed expectations so no one can ever think they can afford you. This means putting in more effort than what is required. I do not remember working at a job where I gave all that was required, I always gave more.

It's all about avoiding the trap of being average but to excel, you have got to take risks. Sure, fear can hold you back, but think of all the missed opportunities that would result. Take becoming a pilot, for example. Some folks could've done it, but fear got in the way. We cannot let that happen to us. Now, whether rich or poor, we're all made by God. So, if someone's stuck in poverty, it's partly because of what they're doing - or not doing. It's not just about praying; we've got to change our actions too. Look at Solomon, he was definitely not average. He wrote tons of proverbs, which is no small feat. Successful folks own up to their results, good or bad, but sometimes people do it just for the money. Consider Elon Musk; he's been known to sleep in his office to get things done. Then some start a business just to sell it off and live an easy life. They're not interested in adding value; it's all about the cash. That's why you see so many quick-fix restaurants around. They're not about serving people but making a quick buck. That mindset won't last. God's calling us to make a change - in our work, mindset, and everything. He's calling you, and He's calling me. Let's rise to that challenge and make a real difference. Decide to go above and beyond in everything you do.

RESIST RATIONALIZATION

Whoever taught you to question everything (rationalization) has taught you to be poor. It sounds appealing to question everything, but ask yourself: Are the professors advocating this mindset wealthy or financially prosperous? The answer is most likely no. Those who teach us to question everything are attempting to instill a mindset of skepticism, yet it is faith, not reason, that brings blessings. When speaking about worldly concepts, reason prevails. However, in creating what has never been seen, faith is paramount. Without the 'eye of faith,' we cannot receive anything good from the Lord. The opposite of questioning everything is to believe. Faith will always take us beyond where reason can take us. World changers know that faith must be engaged to go further after reason has taken you as far as possible. Reason will help you examine people based on their past, while faith will help you to believe the best in others, even though their best self has not manifested yet. Faith is crucial, and an atmosphere of faith can bring financial blessings.

HONOUR ELDERS

Last but most importantly, whoever taught you to dishonour elders and those in authority has positioned you to be poor. Who is an elder? An elder is someone who has excelled in an area where you have not yet excelled. They can be an elder in grace or an elder in wealth. Therefore, some elders can even be young. *"Do not curse the king, even in your thought; Do not curse the rich, even in your bedroom; For a bird of the air may carry your voice, And a bird in flight may tell the matter."* (Ecclesiastes 10:20)

You cannot draw grace if there is no love and honour. How can someone who desires to be rich be abusing rich people? How can someone who desires to be great be abusing great people? Unfortunately, the culture in some homes is to abuse rich and successful people. When they gather, they abuse. Grace is not only imparted from ministers of the gospel. A wise man said that Nelson Mandela had grace that statesmen or people who wanted to go into governance needed to receive. Nelson Mandela is not the only politician who has been imprisoned because of activism but he has grace that distinguished him.

A culture of dishonour will eventually lead to poverty. *"The blessing of the Lord makes rich and He adds no sorrow to it."* (Proverbs 10:22) It's the Lord that blesses and He is the ultimate authority. You stand a better chance of prosperity when you adopt a principle of honour towards everyone, especially elders. Even Abigail's husband in the Bible who was dishonourable to David would have had to honour some people to get to where he got to. Elders are custodians of principles. You cannot dishonour elders and expect to capture their principles and enjoy their grace. Elders are gatekeepers. They might not have what is inside the gate, but they are gatekeepers. Even though Naomi was single, she knew how to arrange a husband for Ruth. Some people erroneously believe that an elder has to be rich to make others rich. The level of honour we are being asked to display in Ecclesiastes 10:20 is extended even to our thoughts. From today, I beg you, when you see a rich person, except if you know clearly that they got their wealth through illicit means, respect them. It was not child's play for them to have gathered what they gathered. Without honour, there's no impartation. Without impartation, there's no grace because impartation is the giving of grace. Honour is key.

5

The Blessings of The Lord

We serve a good God who desires prosperity for His children. The God of heaven is not interested in making His children impoverished, for He Himself is abundant. The Bible even mentions that the materials used in the New Jerusalem are precious stones.

"The construction of its wall was of jasper; and the city was pure gold, like clear glass. The foundations of the wall of the city were adorned with all kinds of precious stones: the first foundation was jasper, the second sapphire, the third chalcedony, the fourth emerald, the fifth sardonyx, the sixth sardius, the seventh chrysolite, the eighth beryl, the ninth topaz, the tenth chrysoprase, the eleventh jacinth, and the twelfth amethyst. The twelve gates were twelve pearls: each individual gate was of one pearl. And the street of the city was pure gold, like transparent glass." (Revelation 21:18-21)

This picture of the New Jerusalem is evidence that God is not broke. Since we are made in the image of God, we ought to think prosperity and manifest prosperity. Prosperity is not just in money, it is also in relationships. Having people you know can stand with you, come rain and shine, is also prosperity. Many people have thousands of friends on Facebook, Instagram and other social media sites but cannot turn to any of them when there is an issue. Proverbs 10:22 tells us that the blessing of the Lord makes one rich, and He adds no sorrow to it.

Many people in the church have abused the prosperity message, making many people run to the extreme and say, "You know what? I don't want to be rich." Many Christians don't want ministers to talk about money anymore because some preachers have abused the prosperity message. Some Christians say they only want Jesus, but Jesus came with everything good. Beloved, any message can be abused. Even the message of holiness is also abused in some quarters. So, we need to be careful and remain balanced in accordance to the Word of God.

"Then I looked, and I heard the voice of many angels around the throne, the living creatures, and the elders; and the number of them was ten thousand times ten thousand, and thousands of thousands, saying with a loud voice: 'Worthy is the Lamb who was slain To receive power and riches and wisdom, And strength and honor and glory and blessing!'" (Revelation 5:11-12)

Worthy is the Lamb who was slain to receive power, riches, wisdom, strength, honour, glory, and blessing. Jesus received these riches for us, His children. Riches are not needed in Heaven; He received them on our behalf. Personally, I desire every redemptive right in Christ. The Bible says Abraham was blessed in all things, and Abraham and the poor Lazarus made it to Heaven. God desires us to be financially blessed, but it is up to us to accept this by faith and work towards it. We need money to fulfill God's purpose for our lives. We cannot pay our rent by speaking in tongues unless the Holy Spirit instructs us to do so. Nothing is holy about being unable to pay your rent; God wants us to be blessed.

"Thus says the Lord to His anointed, To Cyrus, whose right hand I have held— To subdue nations before him And loose the armor of kings, To open before him the double doors, So that the gates will not be shut: 'I will go before you And make the crooked places straight; I will break in pieces the gates of bronze And cut the bars of iron. I will give you the treasures of darkness And hidden riches of secret places, That you may know that I, the Lord, Who call you by your name, Am the God of Israel.'" (Isaiah 45:1-3)

THE DIVINE PURPOSE OF WEALTH

If wealth were bad, why would God give us the power to obtain it? This power establishes His covenant, which He swore to our ancestors. Wealth is necessary for establishing a covenant, and God will not empower us to acquire something evil, as the Bible states that God does not tempt us with evil. You can be financially blessed and still be holy; you can be financially blessed and still make it to Heaven. The Bible teaches that the love of money is the root of all evil. Do not let the pursuit of money captivate your heart, and avoid checking your bank account obsessively. When God prompts you to give, be generous. Do not become too attached to money. Proverbs 23:5 warns that money will grow wings and fly away if you chase after it. Instead, we should pursue God. Matthew 6:33 advises us to seek first the Kingdom of God and His righteousness.

When we pursue God, riches, goodness, mercy, and all the things others chase after will follow us. These are the biblical guidelines God has given us. He will bless us, but we should not be attached to wealth or be stingy with it. God desires our whole hearts. We need His power to gain wealth because the wealth we seek is often in the hands of the powers of darkness.

"Thus says the Lord to His anointed, To Cyrus, whose right hand I have held— To subdue nations before him And loose the armor of kings, To open before him the double doors, So that the gates will not be shut: 'I will go before you And make the crooked places straight; I will break in pieces the gates of bronze And cut the bars of iron. I will give you the treasures of darkness And hidden riches of secret places, That you may know that I, the Lord, Who call you by your name, Am the God of Israel.'" (Isaiah 45:1-3)

WEALTH IS HIDDEN IN BLESSINGS

There are hidden riches in every land, and everyone who finds wealth tends to keep it concealed, ensuring no one else has access to it. This is why the Bible refers to "hidden riches in secret places." We need the blessing of God, as it is His blessing that makes us rich. The power to obtain wealth lies within this blessing. Throughout this book, we have discussed the importance of working hard, being diligent, using your gifts and talents, and having an overwhelming desire to be a blessing. These are our responsibilities, but God's part is to release the blessing.

Take baking, for example; simply combining flour and sugar does not make the batter rise. You must add a leavening agent, like yeast, to the mixture. The yeast represents the blessing. What happens if you just put yeast in a bowl without any flour? Nothing. When the flour is properly mixed with the right ingredients, and then you add the yeast, expansion occurs. It is important to note that not every hardworking person is rich. The Bible says, "The race is not to the swift, nor the battle to the strong, but time and chance happen to them all" (Ecclesiastes 9:11). God is the one who controls time and chance. The blessing of the Lord upon a person causes time and chance to work in their favour. When we have the right mindset, a diligent nature, an overwhelming desire to be a blessing, and a practice of sowing and giving, God's blessing will lead to expansion.

When you see someone working multiple shifts and unable to attend church for extended periods, it indicates that they may have neglected the role of God's blessing. You can put in a lot of effort without God's blessing, and while you might gather a substantial amount of money for a time, a single significant need can deplete it all at once. This often leaves them back at square one or even worse. But when God's blessing is present, as the Bible says, "The Lord blessed Abraham in all things." You can recognize when someone operates under God's blessing; it is evident in every aspect of their life. The blessing of the Lord is the extra element that makes our efforts prosperous.

There is a time for everything, and things grow with time. Ecclesiastes 3:11 says that God has made everything beautiful in its time. You can plant a rose seed but won't see roses immediately. After some time, the roses will bloom.

When I lived with my family, I observed many construction projects. I saw how long it took to build the foundation. Once the foundation was completed, the framing, drywalling, and other processes were finished relatively quickly. Soon, trucks with appliances and fixtures arrived, and within a few weeks, the buildings were ready for possession. The first few chapters of this book focused on foundational principles that we need to follow. God is faithful and will not disappoint us once we have done our part. The blessing of the Lord is the extra element that makes prosperity effortless. We are not meant to be hustlers or toilers. God does His part while we do ours. Working hard without the blessing of the Lord results in hardship. Here are some things to expect when the blessing of the Lord is upon your life.

Divine Favour

Favour is when we receive things we don't deserve, and that's what the blessing does. Some favours are asked for, while others come unexpectedly. God's favour makes people inclined to do things for you. When God's blessing is upon you, favour follows you everywhere. As Psalms 23:6 says, "Goodness and mercy follow you all the days of your life." With God's blessing, favour should accompany you wherever you go.

Joseph's life is a prime example of such favour. The story of Balaam and Balak in Numbers 22-24 further illustrates this. King Balak asked Balaam to curse the children of Israel, but when Balaam spoke, he blessed them instead, declaring, "Who can curse whom God has blessed?" Jesus has blessed you, and no one can curse you without cause.

Divine Inspiration (Ideas)

We see in the scriptures how Jacob was harassed and taken advantage of by Laban. If you are under an overbearing boss, report it to God. God can provide ideas for any situation. He gave Jacob inspiration on how to prosper. After Jacob renegotiated his wages with Laban, God showed him a strategy in a dream that led to his prosperity. Divine inspiration ensures that when you are blessed, no one can take advantage of you—unless you allow them to. The blessings of the Lord provide ideas for solving problems. Understanding this and receiving it by faith should excite you when facing challenges. These challenges separate the weak from the strong, the blessed from the unblessed, and the children of God from those who are not.

Consider David's encounter with Goliath. David saw an opportunity where others saw only the possibility of death. Many inventors, like Isaac Newton, were Christians who attributed their groundbreaking ideas to divine inspiration. Divine inspiration guides us through challenges and leads us to remarkable solutions. When you recognize what you carry, you don't shy away from problems, because God uses them to announce you, showcase your unique contributions, and ensure that your voice is essential in any collective decision-making process.

Protection over God's Blessings

The blessings of the Lord protect our wealth even during a famine. Anyone can be wealthy, but without the blessing, they risk loss.

Malachi 3:10-11 says, *"Bring all the tithes into the storehouse, That there may be food in My house, And try Me now in this, Says the Lord of hosts, If I will not open for you the windows of heaven and pour out for you such blessing that there will not be room enough to receive it. And I will rebuke the devourer for your sakes, So that he will not destroy the fruit of your ground, Nor shall the vine fail to bear fruit for you in the field, Says the Lord of hosts."*

Without the blessing, the devourer can access a person's wealth anytime. However, for the children of God, the Lord will rebuke the devourer for our sake. When the devourer comes, God declares, "Touch not my anointed." In Job chapter one, the Bible says that God put a hedge around Job and everything he owned, protecting it from the devourers. This is the advantage of the blessing. So, when you know you are blessed, do not fear famine. Throughout history, even during economic crises, people have become millionaires, received promotions, and gotten bonuses. The blessings of the Lord protect our wealth, even in times of famine.

Divine Wisdom to Compete

This wisdom is crucial in navigating the world's complexities, which, while we are not living in the Wild West in its entirety—where the law of "kill or be killed" prevailed—is still brutally competitive on an economic level. Indeed, the wealthy, as statistics have shown, continue to amass greater fortunes, and they gain access to information that further enhances their wealth. However, when the blessing of God is upon us, as it indeed is, He provides us with the wisdom to compete with those seemingly greater than us. This divine wisdom can manifest in various forms. For example, in real estate, it is well-known that properties near amenities like Walmart or train stations appreciate in value. Information about future developments, such as a new train station, may be restricted to those with connections to influential figures like mayors or councillors, who can act on this knowledge swiftly.

As Christians, divine intervention can guide us in such ways. A voice in the night might instruct, "Hey, my daughter, wake up. See that part of the land? Go and buy that land there." Without hesitation, you obey. This wisdom to compete is a divine insight that positions us advantageously. As people visit and marvel at our foresight, questioning, "Who do you know? How did you know something was coming?" we can only respond with humility. Our knowledge did not come from human connections but from a higher power. It will be clear that God is actively working in our lives, endowing us with the wisdom to compete and succeed in ways that leave others wondering, "How did you know?"

Multiplication of Wealth

Jesus multiplied wealth when He multiplied the five loaves and two fishes because He was blessed. Proverbs 4:18 says, *"But the path of the just is like the shining sun, That shines ever brighter unto the perfect day."* For children of God, we keep going higher and higher as long as we walk in line with God. Everything a blessed person gets involved in is blessed. We often see worldly millionaires or billionaires transfer their wealth to their children, who destroy their legacy and squander it. Only in a few cases have we seen children of very wealthy people continue on the legacy, preserve the wealth, and even multiply it.

"And it came to pass, after the death of Abraham, that God blessed his son Isaac. And Isaac dwelt at Beer Lahai Roi." (Genesis 25:11)

After Abraham was gone, God transferred the blessing to Isaac. The Bible says when Abraham died, God blessed Isaac. The blessings of the Lord make your wealth transgenerational. The legacy is thus preserved, enduring through generations.

HOW TO GAIN ACCESS TO THE BLESSING OF GOD

We gain access to the blessings of God when we become born again, and Jesus grants us access to the blessings of Abraham, as outlined in Galatians 3:26-29.

"For you are all sons of God through faith in Christ Jesus. For as many of you as were baptized into Christ have put on Christ. There is neither Jew nor

Greek, there is neither slave nor free, there is neither male nor female; for you are all one in Christ Jesus. And if you are Christ's, then you are Abraham's seed, and heirs according to the promise." (Galatians 3:26-29)

This passage emphasizes that through faith in Jesus Christ, we all become sons of God and heirs to Abraham's promise, without distinctions of race, status, or gender. Many discussions about the blessing reference Old Testament figures like Abraham, Isaac, and Solomon. However, in the New Testament era, the moment we accept Jesus Christ, we align with a new covenant. The Bible clarifies that upon coming to Christ, we are granted access to the blessings of Abraham. Yet, some may question why they do not see these blessings manifesting in their lives. Galatians 3:5-9 highlights that miracles and blessings are the results of faith. Just as Abraham believed in God, and it was counted to him as righteousness, we, too, are considered Abraham's descendants and blessed through faith.

"And the Scripture, foreseeing that God would justify the Gentiles by faith, preached the gospel to Abraham beforehand, saying, In you all the nations shall be blessed. So then those who are of faith are blessed with believing Abraham." (Galatians 3:8-9)

So then, we gain access to the blessing by faith through hearing. Without the hearing of faith, nobody can gain access to the blessings of Abraham. Therefore, when you hear an authority tell you that you are blessed, take it as the equivalent of God appearing to you as He did to Solomon; receive the word and believe that you are blessed. The faith in the blessing increases your confidence in the blessing, and it begins to manifest. Those who are saved became saved because they heard the message of salvation and believed. Salvation is by faith, just as the blessing is by faith. We gain access to the blessings of Abraham by faith and not by works. With the heart, we believe, and with the mouth, confessions are made. For example, you can say, "I believe in God." "I am not cursed." "I am blessed." "Everything I touch is blessed because the blessing of God is on me."

"Now I say that the heir, as long as he is a child, does not differ at all from a slave, though he is master of all, but is under guardians and stewards until the time appointed by the father. Even so we, when we were children, were in bondage under the elements of the world. But when the fullness of the time had come, God sent forth His Son, born of a woman, born under the law, to redeem those who were under the law, that we might receive the adoption as sons. And because you are sons, God has sent forth the Spirit of His Son into your hearts, crying out, "Abba, Father!" Therefore you are no longer a slave but a son, and if a son, then an heir of God through Christ." (Galatians 4:1-7)

Remaining in The Blessings of God

One of the reasons we should avoid sin is because it disconnects us from the blessings of God. You see, God forgives, allowing us to make it to Heaven once we seek forgiveness. However, when we sin, we disconnect from God's blessings. The Bible states that we cannot remain in sin and expect God's grace to abound (Romans 6:1). Some attempt to enjoy the best of both worlds. They place one leg in the world and one leg in Christ. This inconsistency is highlighted in the Book of Revelation, where we are told that God despises those who are lukewarm, i.e. neither cold nor hot (Revelation 3:15-16). Moses told the children of Israel to choose between life and death, asking them to choose life, even though the option to choose death exists (Deuteronomy 30:15).

Anyone who tries to 'enjoy' both worlds will not enjoy the full blessings of God. The Bible teaches that we cannot serve two masters, and it is important to align with God firmly. Some people have the idea that embracing salvation means adopting a restrictive lifestyle, but these misconceptions are baseless. In reality, life in Christ is fulfilling and enjoyable. God satisfies His children with good things. The rewards are enriching and fulfilling for those who fully embrace a life with God.

6

Manifesting Prosperity

Let me remind you that prosperity is spiritual. Do not be misled into thinking that money lacks a spiritual foundation. Spiritual people do not ignore money, even though they don't love it. When Jesus was in the temple, He observed the offerings and noted that a woman gave more in the spirit than all the others because He was looking at it. If anyone claims Jesus is not concerned about money, they are either ignorant or deceitful, thus misleading you. Money is crucial for fulfilling your life's purpose. We must ensure that it does not control our hearts, and one way to do this is by being consistent givers.

Partnership with Spirits

The eagle can embody its nature and perform eagle-like activities because it partners with the wind. This partnership offers assistance that, while not visible, is perceptible. There is a realm of prosperity where events unfold beyond direct human intervention. Let's remember this to avoid misinterpreting the message. Hard work and diligence are crucial, but while some rely solely on hard work, others blend it with spiritual investments.

I recently heard one of Africa's billionaires, Ibukun Awosika, speak. She mentioned that whenever she enters a new business environment to close a deal, she removes her shoes to ensure her feet touch the ground and then makes declarations. She ensures her actions align with her understanding, believing she will possess it by stepping on the land. Many successful people understand the importance of spiritual elements. Partnering with the spirit elevates individuals to a magnetic realm of wealth, like a river drawing water from all sources—this partnership draws wealth from everywhere.

If you are pursuing something, ensure you understand it. Some may lack specific business or technical skills and need to rely solely on the spiritual route to prosperity in God. Integrating spirituality is advantageous even for those who believe they possess skills.

How to Identify Those Who Have Partnered with a spirit

A realm of magnetic prosperity results from a partnership between a person and a spirit. The spirit has an agenda and seeks someone to partner with to fulfill it. Consequently, money flows in response to this partnership. People have partnered with a spirit of prosperity because they have a clear and consistent agenda that is unwavering and steadfast. For some, the agenda might be to encourage alcohol consumption or marijuana use. We know of some secular rappers who were once very poor, but now people would even buy their breath packaged in a ziplock bag. This demonstrates a partnership with a spirit.

There is always an agenda for those who have partnered with a spirit. The spirit seeks individuals who can fully submit to it before releasing wealth to implement that agenda.

Partnership with the Holy Spirit

Prosperity is a partnership with a spirit, and every spirit has an agenda. We don't partner with a demonic spirit; we are partners with the Holy Spirit. When we partner with the Holy Ghost, the agenda will be everything God wants to do on the earth, and He will supply the resources for it. You cannot be a pipe with water passing through and remain dry; it's impossible. People who tithe and give get good jobs and will be comfortable above and beyond their means, but in the realm of partnership, money gravitates toward you.

Do you know that even winning souls require money? The more the soul-winning endeavour, the more resources will be needed. When we ask for redemptive blessings, we must also be able to focus on riches. There's nobody today who will say, "Stop preaching about wisdom. Foolishness is good. What's wrong with foolishness?" Nobody will ever say that. But when you talk about riches, they become uncomfortable and say, "Pastor is talking too much about money. Let's move on and talk about winning souls, which are the true riches. Or let's talk more about heaven instead of how to prosper."

"saying with a loud voice: 'Worthy is the Lamb who was slain to receive power and riches and wisdom, And strength and honor and glory and blessing!'" (Revelation 5:12)

The Lamb of God was slain to receive power, riches, wisdom, strength, honour, glory, and blessing. He was crucified so that we can get *all* these things, not some. So, why are we not being allowed to get riches?

Pursuing Boundless Wealth

The realm we must strive to reach in our lifetime is where nobody can quantify our wealth. We must always be grateful but unsatisfied with where we are at every point in time. I learned that about power. For example, you must never be satisfied with your level of power. You must crave more. I learned from Kathryn Kuhlman that there must always be a desire for more, which should be the same with riches.

"And my God shall supply all your need according to His riches in glory by Christ Jesus" (Philippians 4:19)

For more to be supplied, you must want more. You will be supplied to the extent of your need. Many givers and lovers of Jesus are not aware that their low level of supply is because of their low desire for more resources. Can you imagine how much will be supplied to you if you make others' needs yours? Our job is to ensure we have needs so the supply never ends. These needs are not meant to be personal. It must be others' needs that you have taken upon yourself and are ready to distribute as the Lord leads you.

I have watched documentaries of rich people who own 100 cars and all kinds of Rolls-Royces. If that is where your heart is, you will live an extremely sad existence because you will never be satisfied. Will Smith once said that he finally discovered that after you have made so much money and can afford everything you want, you will realize there is no happiness in material things. When you buy a brand-new car for the first time, you will be excited by the scent, the drive, the sound system, etc. I can assure you, however, that after a while, you will forget the car's uniqueness because of life's pressures and responsibilities.

Our needs must be big enough and attached to the needs of the Kingdom of God because nobody can satisfy those needs except God. He will keep bringing more resources to satisfy those needs. Allow God's needs to become your own. Some families at CCCG were financially blessed during the church building renovation process because they took on the Kingdom's needs as their own, and God supplied them accordingly.

Genuine Desires and Abundant Provision

The need in your heart is obvious to a Spirit. When God checks your heart, your genuine need is obvious to Him. King Solomon wanted wisdom to meet God's needs, and his genuine desire was obvious to God. What is the genuine need in your heart? That is what God will supply according to His riches. Why do you desire wealth? Don't limit your aspirations by thinking only of helping yourself and your immediate family. While that's commendable, it's crucial to think far beyond that.

If you make the needs of the whole of Edmonton yours, imagine the resources that will come to you. If you make only your father, mother, and family your needs, then that's the little resources that will come. The Bible says God gave Solomon a largeness of heart (I Kings 4:29), so it is no wonder he had a largeness of resources.

My wife and I attended a conference in 2016, and the first son of Bishop Abioye, a man of God I honour greatly, was present. Just seeing his son alone, we knew we had to send some money to his father through him. This is that realm - where, whether you are physically present or not, people will strongly feel the need to bless you because you have made Kingdom needs your own needs.

"Also I heard the voice of the Lord, saying: 'Whom shall I send, And who will go for Us?' Then I said, 'Here am I! Send me.'" (Isaiah 6:8)

According to scripture, they were in a congregation in Heaven, and there was a call: *"There's a need. Who can we send?"* And Isaiah said, *"Here I am, send me."* That's the same thing with the mission of the spirit of prosperity. Anyone who accepts the call will be sent and empowered with the money to match the extent of the assignment.

ALIGN YOUR ASPIRATIONS WITH GOD'S WILL

Some people seek to support their pastors, church buildings, missionaries, and seniors, while others want to sponsor children's education or assist the homeless. It's important to start somewhere to show your genuine intentions. You might not be able to build housing for those in need yet, but perhaps you can help with part of their rent.

Make your needs significant but take steps according to your current capacity. The pain of wanting to do good but being unable to afford it is part of the anointing that attracts resources to you. Healing ministers understand this principle in relation to the healing anointing; they allow themselves to feel others' pain to generate the anointing. Don't suppress the pain of unmet needs; it's part of the process.

A CCCG member shared that she was in court with her mother and saw people losing their possessions because they couldn't pay their bills, including seniors. This deeply affected her. I told her to keep that agitation and pain and to aspire to a day when she could step into a court and pay off debts for those facing repossession. We know men of God who, through partnership with the spirit of prosperity (the Holy Spirit), fund scholarships for thousands of students they have never met. The greater the need, the greater the supply.

The Principle of Giving

In exploring prosperity, we have encountered various principles and practices that serve as pillars on our journey toward abundance. Among these, tithing, offerings, sacrificial giving, giving to spiritual authorities, and giving to those in need stand out as foundational aspects of our commitment to stewardship and generosity. I will examine them in the order of importance.

Tithing

Tithing, as outlined in Malachi 3:10-12, involves bringing a portion of our income into the storehouse of the Lord. It is a tangible expression of our trust in God's provision and a demonstration of our obedience to His commands. Through tithing, we open ourselves to the abundant blessings promised by God, including protection from the devourer and recognition of our blessed status among the nations.

"Bring all the tithes into the storehouse, that there may be food in My house, and try Me now in this, Says the LORD of hosts, If I will not open for you the windows of heaven and pour out for you such blessing that there will not be room enough to receive it. And I will rebuke the devourer for your sakes, so that he will not destroy the fruit of your ground, nor shall the vine fail to bear fruit for you in the field, Says the LORD of hosts; And all nations will call you blessed, For you will be a delightful land, Says the LORD of hosts." (Malachi 3:10-12)

Offerings

As highlighted in Proverbs 11:24-25, offerings go beyond the obligatory tithe and reflect the generosity of spirit that characterizes a faithful steward. We are to bring something along when we appear in God's house. It is called a free-will offering because we determine an amount to bring to a particular service.

"There is one who scatters, yet increases more; And there is one who withholds more than is right, But it leads to poverty. The generous soul will be made rich, And he who waters will also be watered himself." (Proverbs 11:24-25)

Sacrificial Giving

Sacrificial giving, exemplified in the story of Abraham's willingness to offer his son Isaac in Genesis 22:15-18, transcends mere monetary value. It involves surrendering our most cherished possessions or desires as an act of devotion and trust in God's provision. In return, God promises to multiply our blessings and extend His favour to future generations. God can call for sacrificial giving as He did with Abraham. An individual can also decide to sacrifice to God like Solomon did, as a form of thanksgiving or an act of faith in anticipation of a miracle.

"Then the Angel of the LORD called to Abraham a second time out of heaven, and said: 'By Myself I have sworn, says the LORD, because you have done this thing, and have not withheld your son, your only son — blessing I will bless you, and multiplying I will multiply your descendants as the stars of the heaven and as the sand which is on the seashore; and your descendants shall possess the gate of their enemies. In your seed all the nations of the earth shall be blessed, because you have obeyed My voice.'" (Genesis 22:15-18)

Giving to Spiritual Authorities

Giving to spiritual authorities is giving to biological and spiritual parents as a form of honour for their labour of love over your life. As stated in 1 Corinthians 9:11 and 1 Timothy 5:17-18, those entrusted with teaching and leading within the church are worthy of support and recognition for their efforts.

"If we have sown spiritual things for you, is it a great thing if we reap your material things?" (I Corinthians 9:11)

"Let the elders who rule well be counted worthy of double honour, especially those who labour in the word and doctrine. For the Scripture says, 'You shall not muzzle an ox while it treads out the grain,' and, 'The labourer is worthy of his wages.'" (I Timothy 5:17-18)

"Let him who is taught the word share in all good things with him who teaches. Do not be deceived, God is not mocked; for whatever a man sows, that he will also reap. For he who sows to his flesh will of the flesh reap corruption, but he who sows to the Spirit will of the Spirit reap everlasting life. And let us not grow weary while doing good, for in due season we shall reap if we do not lose heart. Therefore, as we have opportunity, let us do good to all, especially to those who are of the household of faith." (Galatians 6:6-10)

Giving to Those in Need

Lastly, giving to those in need demonstrates our compassion and solidarity with the less fortunate members of society. Proverbs 19:17 reminds us that lending to the poor is akin to lending to the Lord Himself, and Psalms

41:1-3 assures us of God's provision and protection for those who consider the needs of others.

"He who has pity on the poor lends to the LORD, And He will pay back what he has given." (Proverbs 19:17)

"Blessed is he who considers the poor; The LORD will deliver him in time of trouble. The LORD will preserve him and keep him alive, And he will be blessed on the earth; You will not deliver him to the will of his enemies. The LORD will strengthen him on his bed of illness; You will sustain him on his sickbed." (Psalms 41:1-3)

In conclusion, our journey toward prosperity is intricately linked to our willingness to embrace the principles of stewardship and generosity outlined in God's Word. As we commit ourselves to tithing, offering, sacrificial giving, sowing seeds to spiritual authorities, and extending a helping hand to those in need, we position ourselves to receive the abundant blessings God promises to pour upon His faithful children. May we continue to walk in obedience and faith, trusting in God's provision and sharing His love with the world around us.

HEAR & SPEAK ABUNDANCE

The abundance that will manifest in our hands must have been in our heart and declared with our mouth. Everything supernatural begins in the spirit, then downloaded into the heart before the mouth declares out of the abundance it has received. Anything of value can be created if a stirred-up spirit is willing to declare it. There is a deep connection between faith, the heart, and the mouth. That connection goes both ways. This means you can determine faith in the heart by what the mouth says and expect the mouth to speak right because of faith in the heart.

How to Cultivate and Strengthen Your Faith

You might be wondering, "How can I grow my faith?" I am glad you asked. The Bible clearly tells us that *"Faith comes by hearing and hearing by the word of God"* (Romans 10:17). You cannot grow faith by binge-watching things contrary to God's word. The word of God that you take in can either be raw (reading the Bible), the word you cooked (the word God speaks to you), a word someone else cooked (a rhema or preaching by someone else), or a buffet (a testimony of God's word becoming flesh in someone else's life). Your faith will grow exponentially if you make what you listen, read, or watch mainly revolve around these categories. You will see your words change and become more positive. You will notice that you are no longer negative-minded, a pessimist, or a speaker of negative words. A pessimist is a person bankrupt of faith. Why are we talking about faith? Remember that without faith, we cannot please God (Hebrews 11:6).

If the financial abundance we seek comes from God, we must follow His principles and preferences to please Him. Faith is one of such preferences. To receive anything valuable from God, faith must be in operation. As stated earlier, it is not difficult to build faith. The materials are easily available and accessible. Adjust your environment immediately to ensure you constantly hear faith-filled and faith-filling substances. The mouth can only consistently speak what the heart is full of.

"But you, son of man, hear what I say to you. Do not be rebellious like that rebellious house; open your mouth and eat what I give you." (Ezekiel 2:8)

The prophet Ezekiel allowed himself to eat the word of God before he could consistently speak the word of God. In another instance, Ezekiel was told to feed his belly with the word of God. Do you struggle to speak the word? It is most likely because you are not full of God's word. This should be good news because now you know that demonic forces are most likely not hindering your ability to speak the word. If Ezekiel did not open his mouth to eat the word, he would not have been able to speak the word.

"So I opened my mouth, and He caused me to eat that scroll." (Ezekiel 3:2)

"And He said to me, 'Son of man, feed your belly, and fill your stomach with this scroll that I give you.' So I ate, and it was in my mouth like honey in sweetness." (Ezekiel 3:3)

Your Inner Circle's Impact on Faith and Prosperity

A significant aspect of your environment that must be enhanced is the people who speak to your heart. The people around us, especially those with access to our hearts, can determine how far our faith will go. A common saying goes, "Show me your friend, and I will tell you who you are." Those in your inner circle will determine what is in your inner life. Ultimately, you will seek to please those in your inner circle. Those you allow into your heart already control your life. Some people attend church regularly but do not allow the life in the church to permeate them. If you want to increase the faith in your heart, be intentional about the people you behold and those you allow to speak into your life and situation.

It is almost impossible to believe that God cannot bless people, yet you want to be blessed by God. You cannot think that every rich person is a thief, yet you want to be financially prosperous and join the company of "thieves." The state of your heart will determine the state of your life. I grew up seeing people antagonizing every rich, prosperous, and wealthy person they saw around them without trying to understand their story. I made up my mind not to join such people, and you can do the same, too.

Declarations of Faith

Fill your heart with faith in God's desire and ability to cause you to prosper, and let your mouth declare the abundance of such possibilities. I recommend the *Declare album* by Emmanuel Adewusi for spirit-filled and biblically sound declarations, including declarations on financial prosperity.

We understand from scripture that each person will be satisfied based on the nature of their declarations.

"A man will be satisfied with good by the fruit of his mouth, And the recompense of a man's hands will be rendered to him." (Proverbs 12:14)

"A man shall eat well by the fruit of his mouth, But the soul of the unfaithful feeds on violence." (Proverbs 13:2)

After you have applied the principles outlined in this book, ensure you are also declaring the right things. If your bank account is not lining up with the will of God, speak the will of God instead of your reality. Your declarations are more potent when said regardless of the prevailing situation. The reason for this is that it would have taken so much faith to declare the will of God despite your situation.

The Bible says, *"...let the weak say, 'I am strong'"* (Joel 3:10). If you find it challenging to speak life even after reading this book, cleaning up your environment, saturating your mind with the word of God in various forms and also testimonies, you can take it to God in prayer. In Daniel 10:16, Daniel recounted how his speech was enhanced after the divine personality touched his lips. May the Lord touch your lips now, in Jesus' name.

"And suddenly, one having the likeness of the sons of men touched my lips; then I opened my mouth and spoke, saying to him who stood before me, 'My lord, because of the vision my sorrows have overwhelmed me, and I have retained no strength.'" (Daniel 10:16)

Epilogue

As we wrap up this journey through financial prosperity, I am thankful for the opportunity to share this experience with you, dear reader. Together, we have explored the depths of God's abundant provision and unearthed the timeless principles that pave the way for a life of abundance and fulfillment.

We've delved into scripture, uncovering principles that help unlock God's financial blessings. From the stories of Abraham, Isaac, and Jacob to the wisdom of King Solomon, we've gained valuable insights into the divine principles of prosperity.

But our journey does not end here. I encourage you to continue to embrace financial prosperity and share it with others. Let's be ambassadors of God's abundance, living examples of His faithfulness and provision.

I hope this book inspires transformation in your life, helping you embrace the abundant life God has planned for His children. As you walk in obedience and faith, may you experience the overflowing blessings of His grace and the fulfillment of His promises in every area of your life.

Remember that you are not alone in every step of this journey. Your Heavenly Father walks beside you, guiding you with His wisdom and empowering you with His strength. Trust in His provision, lean on His promises, and rejoice in the abundant life He has prepared for you.

Remember that you are cherished and celebrated as a beloved child of God, destined for greatness and prosperity beyond measure. May His blessings continue to overflow in your life, now and always. I will hear your testimony of divine wealth in Jesus' name.

Contact the Author

I know without a doubt that this book has been a blessing to you. I am looking forward to hearing your testimony.

You can stay connected with me through the following platforms:

Instagram: e.adewusi | **Youtube:** Emmanuel Adewusi
Website: emmanueladewusi.org

SUPPORT THE AUTHOR

Review the Book

A Sinner's Prayer

Dear Heavenly Father,

I come to You in the Name of Jesus Christ.

You said in Your Word, "Whosoever shall call upon the name of the Lord shall be saved." (Romans 10:13) I am calling on Your Name, so I know You have saved me now.

You also said that "if you confess with your mouth the Lord Jesus and believe in your heart that God has raised Him from the dead, you will be saved. For with the heart one believes unto righteousness, and with the mouth, confession is made unto salvation." (Romans 10:9-10) I believe in my heart Jesus Christ is the Son of God. I believe that He was raised from the dead for my justification, and I confess Him now as my Lord and Savior.

Thank you, Lord, because now, I am saved!

Thank You, Lord, because I know you have heard my prayer. Thank You, Lord, because I am now born again.

Signed _____

Date _____

About the author

Apostle Emmanuel Adewusi is the Founding and Lead Pastor of Cornerstone Christian Church of God.

Called into ministry with the mandate to "bring restoration and transformation to all by teaching, preaching, and demonstrating the Gospel of Jesus Christ," he is passionate about seeing lives restored and transformed as God intended from the beginning of creation. He has a zeal for the full counsel of the Word of God, fellowship with the Holy Spirit, and being under spiritual authority.

He authored the books *"Now That You Are Born Again, What Next?"*, *"The Blessings of Being Under Spiritual Authority,"* *"A Disciplined Life,"* *"The Enlightened Believer,"* *"The Skilled Sower,"* and other impactful titles. He has also released an album titled *"Divine Encounter"* and many more on the way.

Emmanuel Adewusi is joyfully married to his wife, Ibukun Adewusi, and together, they are building a thriving Christ-centered family.

www.ingramcontent.com/pod-product-compliance
Lightning Source LLC
Chambersburg PA
CBHW050249010526
44107CB00003B/254